JEAN COCTEAU

JEAN COCTEAU

THE HISTORY OF A POET'S AGE

BY

WALLACE
FOWLIE

BLOOMINGTON

INDIANA UNIVERSITY PRESS

LONDON

For permission to reproduce the drawing and photographs
in this book, we are grateful to M. Edouard Dermit.

To Ronald and Carole

CONTENTS

LIST OF ILLUSTRATIONS

JEAN COCTEAU

I

AT THE POET'S
DEATH

JEAN COCTEAU died in his own house, at Milly-la-Forêt, on October 11, 1963, at the age of seventy-four. During the seventeen years he had been proprietor of the house, he had stored in it objects that had come to him, especially from friends, and for which he had some sentimental attachment. More than his small Paris apartment and more than the villa of Santo-Sospir in Saint-Jean-Cap-Ferrat, the Milly house had become home for Cocteau, a second body for the soul, as he had once called a home. There is a photograph of his writing desk in the Milly house, and it shows the array of photographs of those closest to him and of objects he cherished: Raymond Radiguet, Jean Marais and Edouard Dermit; Sartre and Orson Welles, Picasso, Marlene Dietrich, a bust of Byron, a pair of banderillas, a painting of Mme Francine Weisweiller.

A citizen of Milly-la-Forêt for seventeen years, he deserved the town's homage which he received at his funeral, when all the civic and religious organizations were represented at the procession and the funeral mass. He was buried

3

in the chapel, Saint-Blaise-des-Simples, which he had decorated by painting a series of herbs and medicinal plants
(*simples*) on the inside walls. By the time of his death,
Cocteau had quite literally become the characterization he
had assumed when he signed some of his drawings: *le sire
de Milly*.

Juliette the housekeeper and her husband the gardener
had with great devotion cared for Cocteau when he lived
in Milly. Nearly his last words were to Juliette, when he
said to her he was not well and that she was seeing him for
the last time. *Je ne suis pas bien. C'est la dernière fois que
vous me voyez*. When Cocteau first occupied the Milly
house, in 1947, he employed a young gardener, Edouard
Dermit, who was destined to play an important role in his
life. As an adolescent, Dermit had worked in the iron mines
of Lorraine. When Cocteau discovered his talents as an
artist, he helped make him into a serious painter who today
is painting the frescoes of a small chapel in Fréjus, a work
for which Cocteau had left numerous drawings and sketches.
Dermit played the roles of Paul in the film *Les Enfants
terribles* and Cégeste in *Orphée*. He was adopted by Cocteau
and entrusted with the manuscript of the autobiographical
work, *Passé défini*, to be published posthumously.

When his death was announced, all those who were
familiar with his work, and especially those who, during the
first few weeks following his death, wrote testimonial notices,
remembered the exceptional closeness Cocteau had always
felt for death. In trying to express this closeness, he had
once used the metaphor of a coin and said that life and death
were the two sides of the same coin, separated only by the
thickness of the metal, although they cannot know one
another. He resented all funeral pomp and ceremony. At
Giraudoux's funeral, for example, he grew depressed by the

oratory and display, and said to a friend: "Let's leave. He didn't come." (*Allons-nous-en, il n'est pas venu*.)

In his poem *Plain Chant*, Death is called an evil companion (*mauvaise compagne*), and in *Orphée*, she is a leading character, rubber-gloved in her role of surgeon. For Cocteau, death cohabits with us in close union. We marry her at our own birth, and adjust to her temperament. "She is our youth, our development, our loves." (*Elle est notre jeunesse, notre croissance, nos amours*.) On that Friday in October 1963, Death joined with him in perfect union, and the poet took his place between the schoolboy Dargelos and the angel Heurtebise. Suddenly he became, for all those who had been following his gyrations and accomplishments and who had never been able to see clearly who he was, a permanent figure with more visible features.

His death marked the beginning of a new era, as it does for every artist, when the work exists alone, when the accidents and adventures of living can no longer affect the work. Too often it was said—and always derisively—that Cocteau's masterpiece was his life. He suffered more than most from this type of judgment and from the legendary character created out of the facility with which he seemed to work and the alleged fickleness and even dissoluteness of his personal life. "They have made of me a character I would not like to meet," he used to say. (*On a fait de moi un personnage que je n'aimerais pas rencontrer*.) During the first part of his career, he was amused by the lies and exaggerations promulgated around his name, but in the later years they distressed him and he would plead, even with his friends, to be more just toward the man he really was, toward the fundamental traits of his character. *Vous ne me connaissez pas, vous ne savez pas qui je suis, rendez justice enfin à mon vrai visage.* His fame victimized him. The stories about him were far more heeded than his books were read. He accepted this, despite the pain it caused him, with the knowledge that an artist comes into his own posthumously.

The literalness of his death, when it occurred, gave suddenly and unexpectedly a new dimension to his work and to the legends that had grown up around the name of Jean Cocteau. The man who had once mimed his own death in his film *(Le Testament d'Orphée)*, and who had carried on throughout his life a persistent dialogue with the beyond, had reached the definitive rendezvous. At last he had become purely Orpheus. He had passed through the one unavoidable event after which both his detractors and admirers would have to decide whether he had been a clown or a poet. The judgments, the estimates during his lifetime had been disarmingly varied. Was he preeminently the restorer of Greek tragedy, as in *La Machine infernale*, or the author of bourgeois drama, as in *Les Parents terribles?* Was he the classicist, as in his novel *Les Enfants terribles*, or the surrealist, as in his poetry? Was he the type of artist given to overrepeated, overfacile emblems: statues, angels, snow, roses, roosters? Or was he the artist who has articulated the deepest drama of our time, whose entire work is a cry of anguish?

When the motorcycle policemen appeared on the highways around Milly, on October 16, 1963, the friends attending the funeral remembered the scenes from the film *Orphée* when the *motards* in their sinister appearances and disappearances created one further Cocteau myth. Themes, choreography, graphic profiles are imprints of this artist's sensibility. By his manipulation of such a myth as *Orphée*, he taught two generations that poetry is that power which temporarily wrests life away from death.

Never did Cocteau savor for any length of time a success or an intimation of glory. For fifty years he never stopped working, moving from one accomplishment to another. He never took time out in order to hate or attack. He moved through time swiftly, indefatigably, until his death, and since that event time has been working for him. The most often repeated testimonial to Cocteau from younger writers and artists is the passion for work he communicated to them. His method of work allowed this uninterrupted productivity, because he seized immediately on what was at hand in order to convert it into a form of art. The work was done first and then afterward he might search for its explanation. *On trouve d'abord, on cherche après*—was a basic article of faith for Cocteau. The pure instinct of the artist guided him during the initial stages of creative work.

A few hours before his death he had learned, from his housekeeper Juliette, of the death of Edith Piaf, an artist whose career he had helped to promote. An hour before his death, Cocteau was preparing to receive the visit of a reporter in order to dictate some statement about Piaf. This final gesture of generosity was characteristic of his life. A large part of his work involved the understanding and transforming of many artists and many forms of art. Such human experiences and such aesthetic experiences were calculated to alleviate the monotony of living, but each one always served in Cocteau's work itself, whether it was the airplane of Roland Garros, the making of a film, addiction to opium, playing in a jazz orchestra, the writing of poems or criticism, the staging of a play and even the acting of one of the parts, the writing of a play, choreographing of a ballet. Not only did Cocteau's body remain agile throughout the years so crowded with activity, his spirit also sustained its youthfulness, and this spirit was at the source of his eagerness to experiment, to test every possible expression of art. René Clair, when he learned of the passing of Cocteau, stated that his friend had

Jean Cocteau

died at the end of a long adolescence: *mort à l'issue d'une longue jeunesse.*

The roles he played in life, the public episodes that became chapters in a life story, the long line of artistic successes swiftly attained and quickly abandoned in turn, the friendships with so many famous figures in so many of the arts, make it impossible to choose one part from among so many that will designate Cocteau's permanent contribution. Variousness is the clue to his genius. At sixteen his poetry was read publicly by a celebrated actor of the day. A few years after that Diaghileff addressed Cocteau with the two words which since then have been endlessly repeated as the admonition spoken at the beginning of a career, which was to be faithfully followed: *étonne-moi.* Cocteau did astonish not only Diaghileff but all of Paris, in 1917, with *Parade,* and he escaped from the crowd at the theatre bent on attacking him and doing him bodily harm only because he was protected by Guillaume Apollinaire, who was wearing his uniform, and around his head a heavy bandage. On that memorable night the word *surrealism* was heard for the first time.

When Cocteau played the drums in a jazz band, he helped launch the fashion of jazz. His first film, *Le Sang d'un poète,* initiated a use of *le merveilleux* in cinema art which is still being copied. On meeting the Negro boxer from Panama, Al Brown, he became the fighter's manager and forced him back into the ring, where he recaptured the championship. With *Antigone* and *Orphée,* in which he played Angel Heurtebise in the Pitoeff production, he rejuvenated the theatre of antiquity. He added a new dimension to the art of journalism by undertaking a trip around the world for *Paris-Soir* and communicating his observations to the newspaper. He was among the very first to call attention to the art of Picasso and the art of Louis Armstrong.

He seemed destined to amuse the public, the wrong kind of public, with the long series of "numbers," of adroit performances which constantly brought back his name. Photographed everywhere, at bull fights, at jazz concerts, at social events of Tout-Paris, his face and his name became associated with worldliness, with the quasi-scandalous activities of the newest arts, with reporters and whatever erratic subject they might raise in their interviews. When the highest and most solemn honors came to him, an honorary degree at Oxford, an invitation to lecture at Harvard, membership in the Belgian Academy and the French Academy, it became more apparent that the long career had not been motivated by an ambition to amuse, that underneath the spectacular aspects of his public life, Cocteau was an indefatigable worker, a man believing that a supernatural force always directed the natural forces, an artist whose life work testified to a coherent unity and principle, whose seeming facility was his method of work, his unwillingness to interrupt his work when either success or failure came. In his particular universe no barriers separate one art from another. A momentary failure in one of the arts can be converted into a success in another form of art. The generosity of Cocteau's nature and the intelligence of his mind prevented his lingering over insult or attack or animosity. To love and to feel himself loved were indivisible needs of his temperament, and they lay at the basis of the artist's impulse to create and to justify his life in the eyes of friends and of all those he did not know but looked upon as friends.

II
THE POET'S BIRTH
1889–1914

JEAN COCTEAU came from a strictly bourgeois family. Stockbrokers and admirals were in his background. Concerts were given in the home of his grandparents. His mother and father were theatre-goers. He was born in Maisons-Lafitte, not far from Paris, July 5, 1889, and he grew up in Paris, as a Parisian. His earliest memories have to do with the theatre in some form or other: with the circus, with the ice-palace and the Eldorado, where he applauded Mistinguett. There was the serious theatre too, tragedies performed at the Comédie-Française, by such renowned and histrionic actors as Mounet-Sully, de Max, Sarah Bernhardt. These were gods and goddesses, worshipped by Cocteau as *monstres sacrés*. At sixteen, his first volume of poems, *La Lampe d'Aladin*, was published. Undue attention was given it in a public reading by the actor Edouard de Max, but even at that age, Cocteau sensed the danger of such acclaim and he moved on quickly to other styles and genres. Very early he established the habit of testing a new genre immediately after completing a work.

He was first the product of those years immediately preceding the First World War, 1900-1914, years of refined artistic taste, years which were devoid of political turmoil, untroubled by any fear of invasion, save briefly in 1905. Three literary personalities, all of whom were socially engaging and histrionic—Anna de Noailles, Marcel Proust, and Maurice Barrès—were devoted to the young Cocteau. They were eminences whom he quickly made into friends. They promoted him, but he also, in the flattery and sincerity of his friendship, promoted them. Cocteau's real exploration of the world of the theatre began when he encountered the Ballets Russes of Serge de Diaghileff and such a work as Stravinsky's *Le Sacre du printemps*, first played in May 1913. From then on, the theatre was for him that place where the acrobatic games of the circus are fused with the ritual solemnity of the catacombs.

Cocteau watched Nijinsky create most of his roles. In real life, Nijinsky appeared excessively small in stature, a monkey with an almost bald head, and with overdeveloped muscles. But on the stage, at a distance from the public that idolized him, he turned into the handsome figure of a dancer. He appeared taller and thinner than he really was. He was the type of artist who never interrupted work on his roles, who continued to perfect what the public had acclaimed as perfection. Cocteau remembered especially the endings of two ballets in which Nijinsky danced two poignant death scenes: in *Pétrouchka*, where the puppet grew into a human figure of great pathos, and *Schéhérazade*, where he thrashed about the stage like a fish on the bottom of a boat.

Not only was Cocteau one of the principal actors in the pre-war years of Paris of 1900-1914, he helped more than most in the creation of the arts which characterize that age.

The theatre, in all of its forms, had become a center of social life and art. And Cocteau, even as a child, before the turn of the century, had been drawn toward what he was to call *les monstres sacrés*, those stars who appeared nightly, *la vedette* or *l'étoile*, each of whom was distinguished by his singularity, by his originality. Even as a youngster, at the circus, Cocteau was held by the performances of the acrobats and the tight-rope walkers, performances that seemed to him brilliant acts of defiance, vertiginous efforts to defeat death. The acrobats taught him an early lesson on the histrionics of the theatre, one expression of man's longing to survive a perilous world.

The atmosphere of the theatre became a world for him. He cherished a cult for the heroines of the footlights, for the ceiling chandelier *(le lustre)*, for the mysteriousness of the boxes *(les loges)*, and for the darkness *(la pénombre)* spreading over the house just before the curtain and the three loud knocks *(les trois coups)*. Every detail of a theatre production fascinated him, from the luminously painted back-drop to the women selling caramels in the intermission. In the small concert hall of the Conservatoire he listened for the first time to the music of Beethoven and Berlioz and Wagner. The real theatre, before he experienced it, he had learned to imagine and dream of, especially on those nights when his mother, before leaving for the theatre, bent over him to kiss him goodnight, and he sensed, in her elaborate dress, her jewels, feathers, and velvet, the shining lights of the theatre chandelier and the magic world of metamorphosis. In the circus he cherished the smells, above all, and the net used by acrobats, which he called no-man's land between heaven and earth. At the Nouveau Cirque, he watched the clown Footit, with the grimace of his cruelly-reddened lips, as he enacted all alone the three characters of baby, nurse, and *grande dame*. Footit performed a miniature drama in which all the children present could relive the pranks of growing up and tricking adults.

About 1904, Cocteau watched the first dances imported from America, the boston and the cake-walk, and the first Negro performers, forerunners of American jazz which was to hit Paris a bit later. The elaborate skating rink called Le Palais de Glace des Champs-Elysées was another kind of theatre for Cocteau where he often observed at a table Willy and his wife who one day was to be called Colette, and Colette's bull-dog. Cocteau claimed that Colette at that time resembled a fox in a cyclist's costume or a fox terrier in a skirt. At five o'clock the school children were supposed to go to the dressing room, have their skates removed and be dressed and jostled and taken home by their nurses. They soon realized that the skaters who succeeded them were the *cocottes* of Paris, the lavishly dressed ladies of easy virtue, and actresses. Jean and his playmates would put off as long as possible the moment of their departure in order to watch the invasion of this feminine world of beauty which they sensed it would not be appropriate to discuss with their families.

The eyes of a child, like the snap of a camera, register scenes very quickly, and much later the negative is developed. Cocteau, always attentive to fashion, to what was in vogue, was also attentive to that part of fashion destined to die young, and to that part which was to survive. From the arts prevalent in his early years, he was to witness the passing of Madeleine Lemaire's painted raspberries and the speeches of *Cyrano de Bergerac*; and he was also to witness the survival of Cézanne's art and the music of *Pelléas*. Traces of fashion and convention in his early works, became, before his death, historical elements, accepted as such. *Les demoiselles du téléphone* were, in 1960, creatures of another age. But their convention was necessary to the plot of his play *La Voix humaine*. To replace them with the dial telephone would have ruined the play. The convention was maintained, in its role of an earlier fashion, in much the same way that *Madame* is still maintained in a Racine tragedy.

Cocteau was a bad pupil at every lycée he attended, at Le Petit Condorcet and Le Grand Condorcet and Fénelon. He was always terrified at being called on in class, and foiled in his efforts to read and copy from his neighbor who inevitably surrounded his paper with a wall of dictionaries. His memories of school had a pivotal point, the little street, la cité Monthiers, between the rue de Clichy and the rue d'Amsterdam, close to the entrance of Le Petit Condorcet. It was the scene of the snowball fight that was celebrated in *Les Enfants terribles* and *Le Sang d'un poète*. The story of the snowball fight was true but it was enlarged into its mythic proportions by Cocteau the novelist and cinematographer. The school boy Dargelos was a real person and he bore that very name. He has now become a character in French literature, whereas nothing is known today about what became of the boy Dargelos as he grew up. All trace of him has been lost. He was the worst pupil of the class, but he held first place with the prestige of his handsomeness and strength and boldness. He charmed everyone in the school: pupils, teachers, headmaster, janitor. He was the proudest bully of the school, *le coq du collège*, and he initiated an inferiority complex in whomever he scorned. Years later, after Cocteau published *Les Enfants terribles*, the critics emphasized the fatal snowball thrown by Dargelos in the opening scene of the novel. They spoke of a stone placed in the snowball, but Cocteau always claimed that the stone was useless, that Dargelos in merely shaping the snowball

with his hands, would convert snow into marble. The episode is from Cocteau's school memories, but in its literary
form, it altered the memories. And often Cocteau wondered
where the real Dargelos was, in later years, stripped of his
fable. Dargelos, the character created by Cocteau, became
for readers of the novel, what he had been to some extent
in real life in the class room, a symbol of the violence in
man which society does everything in its power to tame. As
a child, brought up in the wealthy cultivated world of the
Paris bourgeoisie, Jean Cocteau was taken through many
varied scenes and exposed to many experiences which, later
in his work he recomposed and altered according to the
principle of aesthetic re-creation.

The woman of Paris—la Parisienne—both the fashionably
dressed woman attending the theatre, and the actress or the
singer on the stage dominated, to an extraordinary degree,
the early years of the century. She appeared buried under
folds of silk or mousseline. And then, abruptly, a change
came about, induced by such influences as Negro art, sports
for women, Picasso's paintings, a woman who resembled a
man more closely, in simplicity of attire, in athletic litheness
and suppleness. Greta Garbo and Marlene Dietrich represented the new type of woman, the new star, characterized
by what the French, as well as Americans, called "sex-
appeal." The music-hall singer Mistinguett was for Cocteau
and his friends the new type of emancipated woman: half-
vamp, half-gavroche. They watched her from their box at
Eldorado and showered her with bouquets. Years afterwards,
on Mistinguett's triumphant returns to the Paris public that
loved her, she would invite Cocteau to the opening performance, because he had watched her and admired her
through the years. He has described the special design of
eye make-up she used—called *bicyclettes*—a wheel effect of

blue pencil lines over the eye which exaggerated the shadow of the lashes. Mistinguett's voice became for more than a generation of Frenchmen a symbol of Paris, an almost patriotic symbol. In the roles she played, she incarnated not the various characters but herself, the woman of Paris determined to sparkle and to captivate.

One of Cocteau's encounters with the world of the theatre was his admiration for the histrionic actor Edouard de Max, of the Comédie-Française. De Max habitually broke rules and traditions in his art, in the Racinian roles, for example, of Oreste (Andromaque) and Néron (Britannicus). Even in his apartment, which itself was a revelation to Cocteau, he played a kind of role, an emir, a big cat or a panther, stretched out on cushions and furs that seemed to come from his costume of Hippolyte (Phèdre). The apartment was a stage set, parts of which seemed to resemble Faust's laboratory, or the dressing room of the Fratellini clowns, an apartment where volumes of Verlaine and Baudelaire were bound in such a way as to make them look like missals, where lighting came from cathedral candles, where the bathroom looked Pompeian. The legends that de Max played on the stage stimulated his infatuation with costumes and poses. He was one of the first to like the poems of Jean Cocteau, and he read them publicly at the Théâtre Fémina, where he invited the eminent actors and actresses of the day. It was a colorful beginning for the very young poet, and Cocteau had to work hard afterwards to forget this over-facile triumph.

For a brief period of time, in 1912, Cocteau lived in a wing of the Hôtel Biron, on the rue de Varenne, today the Rodin Museum. It was a large building on a park, in the center of Paris. The elegance of the building, of which Rodin occupied the central pavillon, encouraged Cocteau to compare his

fate to that of Baudelaire the dandy, when he lived at the
Hôtel Lauzun. Every night he noticed a lamp burning late
in one window, and years later he learned that it was the
lamp in the room occupied by Rodin's secretary: Rainer
Maria Rilke. When the two men became friends, Cocteau
told Rilke that at the earlier time, he was so bewildered by
facile success, that he could not have realized he was living
beside a real genius who was at that time unknown.

La comtesse de Noailles occupies a high place among the
early celebrated friends whom Cocteau has portrayed in
writing. He does not speak much about her poetry, but
about her beauty, the timbre of her voice, her witticisms,
her capacity for speaking at great length and so engagingly,
that young people would sit at her feet for long periods of
time, and servants would stand in the doorway in order to
listen. It was an actress's performance—Cocteau stresses this
—in the use of her hand, in the use of props: veils, scarves,
necklaces, muffs, handkerchiefs. The words of Anna de
Noailles enchanted everyone, and Cocteau adds that they
enchanted the trees and the stars outside.

She worshipped glory and fame. Cocteau would accuse
her of this weakness by saying that she wanted to become
a bust in her own lifetime but with legs that would permit
her to run about. (Anna, vous voulez être de votre vivant un
buste, mais avec des jambes pour courir partout.) Toward the
end of her life, when she heard of Cocteau's meetings with
Jacques Maritain and of his Lettre à Maritain, she quarrelled
violently with him over religion. As he escaped down the
stairs one day, she brandished a chair and shouted after
him: "It's quite simple. If God exists, I would be the first
to have been told." (Si Dieu existe, je serais la première à
en être avertie.)

Lucien Daudet, son of Alphonse, was a close friend of

Cocteau, and at the Daudets' home, on the rue de Belle-
chasse, he met, among other celebrities, the literary critic
of the day, Jules Lemaître. The taste, the limitations, the
prejudices of Lemaître marked him as belonging to another
generation. When he attempted to read Cocteau's *Potomak*,
he confessed he did not understand a single word. Lemaître
had been one of the rare critics hostile to Rostand's resound-
ing success, *Cyrano de Bergerac*. When he had called the
play *le fermoir de la guirlande de Julie* (the metal clasp on
a volume of 17th century "precious" poetry), he estranged
Rostand. Mme de Noailles tried to bring about a reconciliation by inviting both men to a dinner party in a restaurant
at the Place de la Bastille. Cocteau was present and has recorded the manner in which Edmond Rostand charmed
everyone including Lemaître. When Rostand's monocle fell,
the waiter and the lady cashier rushed to pick up the pieces
to keep as souvenirs of the great man. Lemaître became
angrily irritated as he watched Rostand take out from his
pocket another monocle and offer it to the cashier, and then
take out a third monocle which he carefully placed over his
eye. On burning a hole in the table cloth with his cigarette,
Rostand exaggerated his remorse by asking what he could
do to repair the damage and Lemaître retorted: "Why don't
you just sign the hole?"

III
THE POET'S TRIAL
1914–1930

At the beginning of the war, Cocteau was turned down by the medical board of the army, and served, more or less illegally, as an ambulance driver on the Belgian front. Some of the landscape background he observed at this time was to be utilized in the novel *Thomas l'imposteur*. He befriended the aviator Roland Garros, accompanied him on some of his flight missions in 1915, and dedicated to him the early poems inspired by aviation, *Le Cap de bonne espérance*.

At intervals during the years of 1916-1917, Cocteau entered the world of the new painters in Paris, and the world of those writers who were friends of the painters. He appeared frequently in Montparnasse with Modigliani and Apollinaire, whenever Apollinaire was on leave from the front. He became friends also with the group more closely associated with Montmartre: Max Jacob, Reverdy, André Salmon, Blaise Cendrars. This was probably the time he met Pablo Picasso, whom he introduced to Diaghileff.

Apollinaire was already wearing the light blue soldier's uniform when Cocteau met him. There was never any trace of disagreement between the two men. Apollinaire was lavishly attentive to Cocteau, as he was to all his friends. Cocteau has especially recalled Apollinaire's language in which unusual words would appear familiar, and familiar words would appear unusual. The laughing eyes of the poet seemed to contradict the seriousness of his face, and the priestly gesturings of his hands. Apollinaire's small room on the boulevard Saint Germain was a museum for Cocteau where the walls were covered with the paintings of his friends: Rousseau le douanier, Marie Laurencin, and *fauve* and cubist paintings.

The morning of the Armistice in 1918, Picasso and Max Jacob came to 10, rue d'Anjou, where Cocteau was living with his mother. Apollinaire was gravely ill and the two friends wanted to secure the services of Cocteau's physician. It was too late. Apollinaire died that evening. For Cocteau and for many others, Apollinaire incarnated an important literary and artistic movement in French history. He dazzled everyone by his learned remarks on esoteric topics, and his prophecies (such as his belief that the new artists owed more to Lautréamont than to Rimbaud) often spoken on his walks in Montparnasse.

Apollinaire had asked Cocteau for a poem to print on the program of the first performance of his play, *Les Mamelles de Tirésias*. Cocteau donated *Zèbre* in which he used the word *rue* in the sense of the verb *ruer* (to kick). The cubists, especially Juan Gris, believed that *rue* must be *une rue* and worried about the poem's meaning. Cocteau told this story as an example of a noble historical decade when such a small detail was able to perturb men's minds. Cocteau believed that Apollinaire's magic was based upon the power of "simples," of medicinal plants he picked along the banks of the Seine and the Rhine. Apollinaire's bearing was that of a prelate and yet his spirit was often as innocent as that of a pious child. Both inquisitor and heretic, Apollinaire composed in his character the extremes of human susceptibilities.

When Cocteau met Raymond Radiguet for the first time in early 1919, he could hardly have guessed that this boy, still only fifteen, was to become in a few years a teacher of a new aesthetics, an example and a model for Cocteau and for other artists who quickly grew to esteem his tact and intelligence. But before long, Cocteau did recognize the genius of Radiguet, and encouraged the young writer in his efforts to contradict his age by advocating an aesthetics of simplicity, of classical clarity. Radiguet denounced the tendency of the newer writers and artists to appear original. He cleared away the accretions that had formed over traditional formulas. He followed the example of *La Princesse de Clèves* in the composition of his novel, *Le Bal du comte d'Orgel*. This novel and his first novel, *Le Diable au corps*, were looked upon by Jean Cocteau as extraordinary in the history of the novel, as the poems of Rimbaud were in the history of poetry.

It would be difficult to point out a direct aesthetic influence of Radiguet on Cocteau, but the example of Radiguet counted tremendously for the older man, and when Radiguet died on December 12, 1923, at the age of twenty-one, Cocteau felt deprived of the strength of a directive, bereft of a friendship based upon a constant interchange of ideas and encouragement and enthusiasms. Radiguet had taught Cocteau that an artist should lean on nothing, that the artist's solitude is fertile and indispensable.

During the two or three years before Radiguet's death, 1920-23, Cocteau had become a familiar figure in certain cafés in Paris where he was in the habit of passing from table to table and greeting such friends as Paul Morand, Jacques de Lacretelle, Drieu La Rochelle. Poulenc and Auric often played the piano at one of the cafés, famous for the new jazz and the new conviviality of the early 20's. At times, even such figures as François Mauriac and Jacques Maritain were present. Both Henri Massis and Jacques Maritain, who collaborated on a new magazine, *La Revue Universelle*, sensed the importance and the firm moral tone of Radiguet's *Le Diable au corps*, and were determined to promote the work of the very young writer.

An addiction to opium, brought on by Cocteau's extreme grief over Radiguet's death, necessitated a period of cure. The poet spent sixty days in the sanatorium (Thermes urbains) on the rue de Chateaubriand, and it was there Jacques Maritain paid his first visit to Cocteau. They spoke of Satie who had recently died, and of Radiguet whose second novel was about to be published. Later, at the home of Jacques and Raïssa Maritain in Meudon, Cocteau met a priest, père Charles Henrion, dressed in the white habit of the order of Père de Foucauld. The spiritual direction of this priest and the friendship with Maritain resulted in Cocteau's return to religious practice. The two long doctrinal letters exchanged between the two men: *Lettre à Maritain* and *Réponse à Jean Cocteau*, made public this experience. If Cocteau's religious fervor lasted only a short while, the encounter with Maritain was of prodigious importance for him. It helped him recover from the death of his friend, it enabled him to clarify his thoughts concerning art and concerning the work of some of his contemporaries, and it initiated a new period in his life during which he was to produce two or three of his most important works: the long poem *L'Ange*

Heurtebise, his play *Orphée,* the text and drawings of *Opium,* and finally *Les Enfants terribles,* written in the brief space of three weeks in March 1929.

After the first opium cure, Cocteau spent some time at Villefranche-sur-Mer, at the Hôtel Welcome. This small harbor on the Mediterranean, close to Nice, was a rendezvous for poets. There Cocteau met the stage designer Christian Bérard, and there he wrote *Orphée* and the series of poems entitled *Opéra.* Villefranche and Nice seemed to be the setting for a fable: the larger city with its gardens, flower markets and luxury hotels, its statues and its Russian colony; and Villefranche resembling the stage set of an Italian comedy, with its jazz bands, its balconies of marble and iron, its palm trees, its proximity to Monte Carlo and Vauban's fortress, its harbor with boats from the English or American navy.

After a temporary estrangement, Cocteau and Stravinsky became reconciled in 1926, and Cocteau wrote the text of their collaborative work *Oedipus-Rex.* Stravinsky began composing the music when living in the section of Nice called Montboron, and Cocteau, who was in Villefranche, often visited him at that time. The oratorio was completed in May 1927, and Stravinsky himself directed the première at the Théâtre Sarah Bernhardt on May 30.

Paris, more than Villefranche, was Cocteau's center during the twenties, when he remained close to many of the friends who had survived Apollinaire. Among those he cherished the most was Max Jacob, the poet-painter from Brittany, the son of a Jewish family who had turned Catholic, the close friend of Picasso. Cocteau was delighted by what he considered the Delphic qualities of Jacob's poems, the play on words, the varied sources of his inspiration: the fairy stories from his native Quimper, the seraphim from Noah's

Drawing by Cocteau of Picasso and Stravinsky

ark, the apparitions of Christ in his room on the rue Ravignan and in a movie theatre. Cocteau with deep sympathy observed the awkwardnesses of Max in his behavior, the ridiculousness of his monocle, his ingenuousness, and he applauded the elegance of his friend's words, the skill of his writing. For Cocteau a poetic genius inhabited both Apollinaire and Max Jacob. The wound on Apollinaire's head was the symbol of a star, and he associated it with the yellow star which Max Jacob wore over his heart in the tragic year of 1944. Picasso was the father in this trinity of modern art, Jacob the son, by his martyrdom, and Apollinaire the spirit of the new movement.

From the paintings of Picasso and the poems of Jacob and Apollinaire, Cocteau inherited the important image of the circus with the sawdust floor over which the tight-rope is stretched. From these artists in particular he learned that poetry is a precise art, as difficult to execute as a circus stunt of acrobatics. He learned that poetry is the result of scrupulous search, a way of revealing and transcending despair. It was a lesson for Cocteau on the dangers of classification, on the need to live in accordance with a disconcerting agility. The miracle of Cocteau's example is that he never wasted or fragmented *himself*. Everything counted: his drawings and his poems, the direction of plays, the creation of archetypal films, chapel frescoes, and ballets. His existence was energy, and it was never declamatory. He was detached from his public, but he was accessible to human suffering.

A false legend made Cocteau into an essentially worldly figure, a man photographed at social functions and interviewed by journalists. This aspect of Cocteau's public life counted very little by comparison with his life of service, his generosity, the simplicity of his manners, the vigilance and attentiveness of his nature, the affection he showed to so many. Even at those moments during the early years of his career when he seemed tempted by the frivolity of worldliness, his character was already dominated by a goodness of heart, by an indulgent understanding of human nature. By his example, he preached kindness. He learned to arrest his feelings just before any impulse to blame could arise. Man rarely has knowledge of sufficient reasons for which to blame another human being. We do not know enough concerning the inner life of a fellow man that would permit us to castigate or reprove. We do not know what is inside a house, what is under a roof, what bonds or tensions exist between human beings. Cocteau's qualities of friendliness and sympathy are also evident in his work because as an artist he joined the unusual with the beautiful, the traditional with the new. He tested every form of imprudence, and often discovered that imprudence was a mask for wisdom.

IV
THE POET'S
TESTAMENT
1930–1963

AFTER HIS recovery from the opium addiction, a new period in Cocteau's life began when he moved into a small apartment in Paris at 10, rue Vignon, and when he discovered an overpowering interest in film making. This was a new means of expression for him, a new form of communication, and as with every other interest in his career, he threw himself whole-heartedly into the making of Le Sang d'un poète. This film, which is still shown today, continues to mystify its audiences, but it has reached the status of a classic.

A serious illness in Toulon momentarily interrupted his work. Thomas Mann sent him a message which he received in Toulon and it gave him the spark of encouragement he needed: Vous êtes de la grande race qui meurt à l'hôpital. In 1932 Cocteau completed La Machine infernale, which was to be first performed in 1934. This play is one of his masterpieces, one of the most unified and concentrated of his works. His interest in the painting of Giorgio di Chirico is the central preoccupation in a critical piece of writing, done also in 1932, *Essai de critique indirecte*. It represents a re-statement, a reaffirmation of many of his convictions about art expressed earlier in the collection of essays, *Le Rappel à l'ordre* (1926). With *Les Chevaliers de la table ronde* (1933), Cocteau returned to writing for the theatre, and this time to a medieval subject where Pagan and Christian themes criss-cross.

For *Le Figaro*, during 1934, Cocteau wrote a series of articles, *Portraits-souvenirs*, which were journeys into his past, into his recollections of celebrities he had met and observed. The articles, published in book form in 1935, were a prelude to the real voyage around the world which Cocteau undertook for the newspaper *Paris Soir* in 1936, and which he called, in honor of the Jules Verne character Philéas Fogg: *Tour du monde en 80 jours*. During this voyage he met and befriended Charlie Chaplin. Between March 1937 and March 1938 he wrote a regular column for the Paris newspaper *Ce Soir*, and during the same period undertook the most unusual of his avocations: the role of manager of a world champion prize fighter.

Alphonse Theo Brown was born in 1902 in Panama, and became known as Panama Al Brown. At the age of twenty-six, he won the bantam weight title. He lost this title in Valencia, Spain, to the Spaniard Balthasar Sangchilli. Cocteau met Brown at a time when the fighter had been down on his luck, and drinking, in the night club Caprice Viennois in Montmartre. He urged Brown to undergo a cure in a clinic and then had him trained in Aubigny for a come-back fight on September 9, 1937 at the Salle Wagram. In a series of matches Brown won over several fighters. The return match for the world title was set for March 4 at the Palais des Sports. Cocteau had just finished his play *Les Parents terribles*, and even the sports writers were beginning to call

Al Brown *l'enfant terrible*. Brown and Sangchilli fought all fifteen rounds and Brown won back the championship. Brown himself claimed that this was due largely to the skillful publicity campaigning, the encouragement, and the friendship of Jean Cocteau.

Immediately after the big fight, Cocteau, in an open letter to Brown published in the newspaper, urged the fighter to withdraw from the ring: "You must stop boxing." But Brown insisted on fighting once more, on April 19, 1938, at the Palais des Sports, where he knocked out the fighter Angelman in the eighth round. Cocteau continued insisting that the fighter give up and devised for him a circus act, a kind of shadow-boxing dance. Sportswriters everywhere and Paris journalists accused Cocteau of meddling in matters that did not concern him and launched a series of vituperative attacks. For a while, Al Brown did travel with the Amar Circus and appeared in the act originated by Cocteau. But it was not long before he was fighting again. His last match, in which he was knocked out, was on January 25, 1944 in Panama City.

Al Brown died in April 1951, of tuberculosis, in New York's Sea View Hospital. A policeman had picked him up when he had fallen on 42nd Street in a state of collapse. Cocteau was told of the seriousness of his friend's condition, and he rushed a tape recording to him from Paris to the New York hospital. Brown listened to the tape on the very day he died. Three Negro friends collected money in Harlem for the athlete's funeral.

Two of Cocteau's plays were first performed in 1937: *Oedipe-Roi* and *Les Chevaliers de la table ronde*. In the first Jean Marais played a minor role, and in the second he took the leading role of Galaad. In 1938, *Les Parents terribles*,

admired today as one of Cocteau's finest plays, began its
difficult career. It was refused first by Jouvet. When it was
played at Le Théâtre des Ambassadeurs, the Conseil Munici-
pal tried to have it stopped as representing an affront to
public morality. It moved to another theatre, Les Bouffes-
Parisiens, where it enjoyed a successful run. It had reached
its four hundredth performance when the war broke out.

More and more, Cocteau had been trying to reach a wide
audience with his plays, and at the same time he was attempting to renovate the genre, to create a new kind of
theatre for his day. In 1939, he wrote *Les Monstres sacrés*
for the actress Yvonne Bray, who had played a leading role
in *Les Parents terribles*, and a monologue play, *Le Bel in-
différent*, for Edith Piaf. *La Machine à écrire*, first performed
in 1941, was a play more in the Ibsen manner, on the theme
of oppression and hypocrisy, and markedly a further effort
on the part of the dramatist to find a communication between stage and audience. The intrigue is borrowed from
melodrama, and every character is caught in some form of
deceit. The major female role was created by Gabrielle
Dorziat, who had also played in the earlier *Les Parents
terribles*.

In 1941, Cocteau moved into the small apartment in the
Palais-Royal: 36, rue de Montpensier, which was to remain
his Paris address until his death. Throughout the Occupa-
tion, he was the object of venomous attacks from journalists
and critics and political figures, particularly on the occasion
of the revival of *Les Parents terribles*. Not only was the play
forbidden, but Cocteau himself was subjected to out and
out brutality and indignities. He wrote a series of articles on
the theatre entitled *Le Foyer des artistes*, and a long tragedy
in verse: *Renaud et Armide*, performed at the Comédie-
Française in 1942. In the same year he produced a new film,

L'Eternel Retour, a fairly hazardous enterprise for wartime.

During the first post-war years there was no relaxation in Cocteau's efforts to work in several artistic domains. His new play, *L'Aigle à deux têtes*, was an experiment in melodrama. His new film, *La Belle et la Bête*, was based on the famous fairy story. His new book of essays, *La Difficulté d'être*, is a series of moral considerations of some of Cocteau's most persistent themes.

In 1947, he acquired the house at Milly-la-Forêt (Seine et Oise) where he was to die in 1963, and began work on his film *Orphée*, a work destined to reach a wide audience and destined to continue holding wide audiences to the present. Internationally acclaimed, this film is a summation of a long career, of a period extending between the writing of the play *Orphée* in 1926 and the film in 1947. It is the most spectacular revelation Cocteau ever made concerning his thoughts about the artist.

When in 1950 Cocteau decorated the Villa Santo Sospir in Saint-Jean-Cap-Ferrat, the home of his friend Mme Weisweiller, he began a series of important graphic works that occupied him intermittently until his death: frescoes on the City Hall in Menton, in 1956, and the chapel of Saint Pierre in Villefranche-sur-Mer; the chapel of Notre-Dame in London, 1958, the church of Saint Blaise-des-Simples in Milly-la-Forêt, 1959. At the time of his death he was preparing to decorate the chapel at Fréjus. He left so many designs and drawings for this work, that his adopted son Edouard Dermit was able to carry out the work in close accord with the wishes of Cocteau. For the chapel at Fréjus, consecrated to Notre-Dame-de-Jérusalem, Cocteau had left one hundred and fifty drawings, and Dermit chose approximately twenty from which to do the wall painting. In the execution of this work, he remained faithful to Cocteau's original designs. During

"Hommage aux Gitans." Fresco by Cocteau on one of the walls of La Chapelle Saint-Pierre, Villefranche-sur-Mer. Completed in 1956

the course of his work in the spring and fall of 1964, Dermit profited from the advice and guidance of Picasso, who came several times from his home in Mougins to la Tour de Mare, the section of Fréjus where the chapel stands.

In addition to his chapel frescoes and illustrations for his books (notably *Les Enfants terribles* and *Opium*), Cocteau left portraits of Apollinaire, Satie, Picasso, and Colette, and studies of the sphinx, Orphée, Judith et Holoferne, and the familiar profile half-Greek, half-angelic, which served almost as a signature on many occasions.

The play *Bacchus* of 1951 centered on a profound theme, the reaffirmation of freedom in its encounters with dogma. It was performed by Jean-Louis Barrault in his Théâtre de Marigny. Cocteau's adversaries and in particular François Mauriac (who was present on the opening night and left before the final curtain) tried to find in it examples of religious heresy. Mauriac's exit was widely noticed. In an open letter to Cocteau, published in *Le Figaro Littéraire*, December 19, 1951, he explained his departure and upbraided Cocteau for his mockery of the Church, in the character of the cynical cardinal in the play. A few days later, on December 31, in *France-Soir*, Cocteau answered Mauriac in an open letter every sentence of which began with the words: *Je t'accuse*. He objected especially to the tone of hatred he sensed in the letter and accused Mauriac of respecting the tradition in France that consisted of killing the poets.

Cocteau's work of essayist and chronicler had continued during all this time: in his *Lettre aux Américains* of 1949, written after a brief visit in New York, in the airplane, between January 12-13, taking him back to Paris; in *Maalesh*, the story of a theatrical tour (1949) in the Middle East (Egypt, Palestine, Istanbul, and Athens); in *Journal d'un inconnu* of 1952. After the publication of his poem *Clair-*

Obscur, in 1953, official signs of recognition, one after the other, honored the significance of his career and his art. Already, in 1949, he had been made Chevalier de la Légion d'Honneur. In 1955 he was elected to Colette's chair in the Académie Royale de Belgique, and in the same year, to the Académie Française where he was received on October 20 by André Maurois. Oxford University gave him an honorary doctoral degree in 1956.

By January 1959, Cocteau had completed preparations for the making of his film *Le Testament d'Orphée*. In February the Opéra Comique de Paris presented for the first time his opera *La Voix humaine*, for which the music had been composed by Francis Poulenc. The one singing role was taken by Denise Duval. The original text of this monologue play had been first performed at the Comédie-Française by Berthe Bovy in 1930. A film was made of the play in 1947 by Cocteau and Roberto Rossellini, starring Anna Magnani. In July, in collaboration with Gian-Carlo Menotti, Cocteau presented a short play *(minodrame)* at Spoletto, Italy. In September he began shooting the film, *Le Testament d'Orphée*, in Les Baux-de-Provence. This was interrupted before the end of the year by a visit to London, where he decorated Our Lady's chapel in the French church and recited the part of the chorus in *Oedipus-Rex*, under the direction of Igor Stravinsky.

Such a brief biographical sketch can allude to only a small part of the activities and achievements of Jean Cocteau. His position is not easily classifiable. It is in a no-man's land where all the arts meet—drama, poetry, fiction, criticism—and where they are fused and unified in the visual, the verbal, the moral.

Many critics have claimed that from all of this work only

a mere "atmosphere" will remain, a "style" designating the various periods during which Cocteau lived. But since his death, a new era has begun in which individual works are being reexamined and reesteemed in terms of their form and the expression of their themes. And some of these seem to have the chance of growing into permanent works of their age. It is true that such a work as *Parade*, when cubism appeared on the stage for the first time, is important for the "atmosphere" it created. And *Les Mariés de la Tour Eiffel*, in the same way, is a document on the early years of surrealism.

But the greatness of Cocteau will be seen in the critical interpretation of his essays, in some of his poems, in such a novel as *Les Enfants terribles*, and especially in some of his films and plays. He reconverted the theatre into what it really is: a place of illusion where he was able to expose such an eternal theme as mythomanic man in search of himself. This is the action of Cocteau's *Orphée*, *Oedipe*, and *Galaad*. Man's preoccupation with his death wish is visible in such works as *Le Sang d'un poète*, *Plain Chant*, and *Bacchus*. The theme of *le merveilleux*, or the miraculous, in the most commonplace objects is apparent in *La Belle et la Bête* and *Les Enfants terribles*.

Cocteau often demonstrates in his art that the reverse of what one usually believes is also true: that death is more beautiful than life, that children are wiser than adults, that criminals are nobler than the righteous. And he was also able to demonstrate the power and the surprises inherent in a *boulevard* type of melodrama. In *Les Parents terribles*, one of his best plays and films, a devouring mother kills herself because her love for her son turned her husband toward a mistress who is the son's fiancée. This is Cocteau's version, in Parisian terms, of ancient Greek tragedy.

Throughout his life, he was prodigal in surprises and mystifications, of which perhaps the most unexpected was his admission to the Académie Française, when officially, in terms of his country's tradition, he became an immortal. In October 1964, on the first anniversary of Cocteau's death, René Clair, as representative of the Académie Française, spoke briefly at Milly-la Forêt and claimed he would not be too amazed if Cocteau suddenly woke up and related to his friends his journey in death.

More persistently than most artists of his age, Cocteau was favored by chance. (Rémy de Gourmont used to say that chance is one of the forms of genius.) Whenever success became apparent in any of his enterprises, Cocteau would turn away from it, and move on to something else, to some other adventure that might end in success or failure. He praised the doctrine of disobedience as being one of the necessary impulses of youth. He worked in the realm of art as if he were unaware of interdictions, and as if every form of creation gave him pleasure. He was able to disguise under the appearance of a game his virtuosity, the skill with which he could move from genre to genre.

Already, the facile disrespectful judgments on Cocteau's work are being revised. He is not the illusionist he was once called, he is not the prestidigitator whose art is the result of tricks. Cocteau was not just the bad pupil, but the steady hard worker who wrote on one of his earliest pages that one has to be first a man engaged in living and then a post-humous artist: *il faut être un homme vivant et un artiste posthume.*

He is one of the subtlest interpreters of the twentieth century, one of its most faithful chroniclers. Whatever picture of the age is held up, Jean Cocteau's sharp shrewd profile is there etched in some corner. During the last years of his life when he met with the academicians, in whose company he continued to use the *tu*-form of address as lavishly as he had done in every other activity where he had participated, it was obvious to all those who had voted for his admission that he was a man who loved friendship passionately. Everything enriched Cocteau's existence, friendship with the quiet simple people of Milly-la-Forêt as well as friendship with celebrated academicians. In one of his last poems, *Requiem*, he speaks of his friends who had died as being just beyond the place where he is. He has only to turn his head to see them. Each one had escaped from him as people disappear from sight in a festive gathering. These few lines constitute Cocteau's understanding of the bond that joins friendship and death:

> Mes amis, mes chers amis
> Où la mort vous a-t-elle mis
> Je n'avais qu'à tourner la tête
> Déjà vous étiez où vous êtes
> Et moi seul de l'autre côté
> Chacun de vous me fut ôté
> Comme on se perd dans une fête.

V

THE POET
AS NOVELIST

THUS FAR, little serious attention has been paid to Jean
Cocteau as novelist. The kind of novel he wrote is not unique
to him, but other examples of the genre—and there are several examples appearing throughout the forty year span of
1890-1930—were written by men who reached wide audiences
by writing more traditional novels. Today, in some perspective after the 1950's, with the development of the *nouveau
roman*, the "ironic" or "poetic" novel of Cocteau appears
more legitimately a genre novel, a form of writing that comes
from symbolism, and that is represented in the work of
Barrès, Gide, Valéry-Larbaud, Apollinaire, and André Breton.

Le Jardin de Bérénice of Barrès, first published in 1891, is
far more a sequence of emotions, a series of notations, than
a story. The narrative element is radically reduced in André
Gide's *Paludes* (1895). The art of Valéry-Larbaud is one of
evocation rather than narrative. A whimsical commentary
fills many pages of a typical Giraudoux novel. In the novels
of Apollinaire and in such a work as *Nadja* of Breton, the
ironical emphasis is uppermost, and the narrative itself is a

meandering, the story of a story. These are works that point up the poetry of the incongruous, the startling beauty that can be found in the commonplace, the surreality that is everywhere in the world surrounding us.

As novelist, Cocteau refused the heritage of the nineteenth century. His purpose in writing the way he did was to charm and startle the reader. He proposes enigmas rather than stories. His art is one of sudden contrasts, of association of ideas, of unexpected transitions and interruptions. The novels resemble film scenarios. There are many examples in the texts of the novels of pictures or scenes swiftly sketched and luminous, that could easily be images projected on a screen.

Le Potomak is not a novel, but it might be looked upon as a preliminary exercise in the writing of a novel. It was composed in 1913, when Cocteau worked in seclusion, first at Maisons-Lafitte, then in Offranville in the home of Jacques-Emile Blanche, and in Leysin (Switzerland), where he lived briefly in the company of Igor Stravinsky. The book, first published after the war, in 1919, and dedicated to Stravinsky, is a strange medley of forms: a collection of drawings, prose poems, dialogues. More than anything else, it is a reaction against the literature of the day. The combined graphic and literary parts lead the reader through milieux that recall infernal scenes, Gothic tales, philosophic dialogues, confessions of a strident lyrical nature.

If there is one subject that pervades the entire work, it would be Cocteau's reaction against the picturesque and the sentimental in literature. The monstrous allegorical figures that move about in these pages, bearing such names as Persicaire and Argémone, possibly come from the author's dream world. They provide the basic elements of the incongruous and the unexpected. Artifice is everywhere, not only in the book's typography (Apollinaire's *Alcools* was also of 1913), but in the shocking notations and revelations of memory.

Both *Le Potomak*, composed just before the First World War, and *La Fin du Potomak*, composed in 1939 just before the Second World War, reveal characteristics of Cocteau's fictional style and method. Even brief notations concerning familiar objects indicate the symbolic use to which they may be put. A paperweight, for example *(un presse-papier)* is not merely a crystal object but an intersection of infinities and silences. The unusual names of Persicaire and Argémone were seen once by Cocteau on old bottles *(bocaux)* in a Norman pharmacy. Underlying this collection of aphorisms and drawings and dialogues is a persistent theme of apprehension, stated sparsely and never sentimentally. It is difficult to say what is actually feared, save a general cosmic tragedy, a feeling of time measured out by some invisible machine of the gods. Cocteau also initiates in *Le Potomak* a life-long dialogue with other writers and gives them advice on the development of their art and what to expect from such a calling as that of an artist. Whatever the public reproaches the artist for should be cultivated because that is the artist. *Ce que le public te reproche, cultive-le, c'est toi.*

Only three books of Cocteau can rightfully be called novels in the sense that they narrate an action and a story. But in all three, certain poetic elements of style and technique are predominant. Two of these books were written close together, in 1923: *Le Grand écart* and *Thomas l'imposteur;* and the third, *Les Enfants terribles*, in 1929. Traits of writing, which usually designate a classical style of art, are apparent in the three novels: a logical kind of clarity, simplicity in diction, an impeccable precision that belies a surface directness and may often reveal an unexpected profundity. The text, broken up in brief paragraphs, reminds one of the *verset* and at times an entire chapter will resemble a prose poem.

The three novels are studies of the mutation from adolescence to manhood. *Le Grand écart* is the drama of a first love, the initiation of a school boy, Jacques Forestier, to love and to a disappointment in love. The most moving passages narrate the progress of his despair. There is an almost total absence in the book of any naturalistic description. The brief notations are images or actions or comments that are avoidances of sentimentality in this story of an *éducation sentimentale*. The crisis that Jacques Forestier goes through is deeply personal and painful, but it is composed by Cocteau with the detachment of a newspaper account, of a chronicle that is a mere recording of facts. Throughout the text, the art of the poet is visible in the combination of words, in the coining of phrases that summarize and partially disguise the actions and the thoughts of the protagonist.

The profoundest aspects of the drama are totally hidden, totally concealed within the text. The reserve of Cocteau when he speaks of the heart, is one of the permanent traits in all his work. Already, in *Le Grand écart*, he is telling his readers that real suffering needs secrecy. The brilliant ellipses, the brilliant condensations are means of blinding the reader to the human anguish of the story. The psychological and moral portrait of Jacques Forestier emphasizes the intactness and the purity of a human heart for which such a style was indispensable. The simplicity and the directness of this narrative are the reflections of Jacques' heart which, as the novelist says, was capable of elevating everything it touched (*coeur intact capable d'ennoblir tout*). It is the story of a heart that cannot be compromised. It is not compromised by even the suicide at the end.

Jean Cocteau studied for his baccalaureat in the private school (*la pension*) of a M. Dietz in Paris. M. Dietz bears the name of M. Berlin in *Le Grand écart*, and the atmosphere of the school will be more fully developed at the beginning of *Les Enfants terribles*, where it is an actual lycée. The profound theme of all three novels is the same: the tragic initiation of the adolescent heart when it refuses to change into the compromising heart of a man.

Two very briefly sketched scenes in *Le Grand écart* are the clue to the drama of Jacques Forestier, and they are in fact the clue to every Cocteau hero. At the age of eleven, in a hotel in Mürren (Switzerland), Jacques watched a very handsome couple, a young man and woman in an elevator *(la cage de l'ascenseur)*. Immediately afterwards, when he looked at himself in a mirror, he compared himself to the couple and wanted to die. We had learned in a passage just preceding the elevator scene, that Jacques' own beauty displeased him, that it was ugly to him. And we had learned at the very beginning of the narrative that the destiny of Jacques Forestier was to be wounded forever by beauty.

A second episode, at the age of eighteen, takes place in Venice, at a masked ball, when Jacques has a further intuition concerning the beauty of those around him who are unmasked by the masks, whose beauty is the demonstration of a spectacular city and a spectacular social ritual. At the age of eleven and at eighteen, Jacques Forestier's soul was wounded by the shock of beauty, by such a fatal shock that the rest of his life, unconsciously to a large degree, will be spent in searching for that beauty. The sight of the young couple in the elevator in Mürren had the tragic effect on the boy Jacques that the snowball will have on Paul, in the opening scene of *Les Enfants terribles*.

Jacques of *Le Grand écart*, Paul of *Les Enfants terribles*, and the narrator of *Le Livre blanc*, are of the race of tragic heroes, fatally attracted to a form of beauty that will cause their destruction. After receiving the fatal blow, in the form of a snowball, or an unexpected vision in an elevator, the hero will continue to live as if nothing had happened. But such an experience of beauty is comparable to a wound, invisible and fatal that will not cease deepening until the hero's life is consumed by it. The purity of Jacques and of Paul is intact throughout the brief years they are permitted to live. And they live and act as if they had not been wounded by the powerful prestige of beauty. But the mechanics of the attraction which secretly dominates their lives, counts out the minutes as if it were an infernal machine of the gods.

The theme of death, as important in the writings of Cocteau as the theme of beauty, impinges so closely on the fatal aspect of beauty that finally the themes become identical. The long passage of Jacques Forestier's attempted suicide is an expression of his will to maintain the vision of beauty and not allow it to succumb to the change of time. Jacques, as well as every other hero of Cocteau, knows that a man's life, if it continues, is governed by his intelligence, by his superficial intelligence, which encumbers it with artifices, with all the devious ways the purity of man's spirit is tricked. *Le Grand écart* contains one of Cocteau's striking images of the swiftness of life, or rather the swiftness of death: that of a train carrying all classes of men simultaneously to death. *Malgré la différence des classes, la vie nous emporte tous ensemble, à grande vitesse, dans un seul train, vers la mort.* Those wounded by beauty will wish the speed of such a voyage and exult over it in a self-determined destruction.

Written just a few months after *Le Grand écart*, *Thomas l'imposteur* is Cocteau's novel on the war. Encouraged by the example of *La Chartreuse de Parme*, Cocteau, like Stendhal, has written a war story, an historical novel in which

History is present but not in the role of arbitrary judge. It is the history of a war without the bombast of war, without the forced inflated sentiments of war. In the same way, and at the same time, Raymond Radiguet was to follow the example of *La Princesse de Clèves* in composing *Le Bal du comte d'Orgel*. The year of 1923 was also the year of Radiguet's death.

The war of 1914 is the setting of *Thomas l'imposteur*. Guillaume Thomas is sixteen and encourages in himself dreams of an heroic destiny. He borrows a uniform, appropriates a famous name, de Fontenoy, and claims he is the nephew of General de Fontenoy. Then Guillaume Thomas de Fontenoy begins to live his part of impostor, which is really his dream. He exemplifies for Cocteau the poet who reveals in his art the adventures that every man conceals in himself.

Guillaume Thomas charms everyone. He inspires confidence in those he meets. In the trenches at the Belgian front, he is unharmed. In the game he plays with death, he lives as under a spell. The imposture allows Thomas to live the myth he created for himself and to die as a hero. The war itself is presented as a spectacle seen from the wings of a stage. *Thomas l'imposteur* derives from Cocteau's personal memory of the war when he was in Belgium, at Nieuport, in 1915, with a group of marines *(fusiliers marins)*. It was a time, as he writes in the novel, when the scamps won out over the good pupils *(les polissons l'emportent sur les forts en thème)*. To some extent, Cocteau's own role at the front was based upon a lie. Thomas is in many ways a stylized portrait of Jean Cocteau. The resemblance between the two is probably truer than what an autobiography would reveal.

The style of *Thomas l'imposteur* is more *stendhalien* than

the books of Stendhal. The narrative moves swiftly, in a
form that is elegant and precise and reserved in its expres-
sions of feeling. The formula used by Stendhal to describe
the art he wanted to create would apply to the art of Cocteau: a story in which everything would be simultaneously
true and ideal (*où tout fût à la fois vrai et idéal*). The total
absence of sentimentality in *Thomas l'imposteur* provides
the book with the evenness of gray and white throughout
the narrative. The tone of irony is present but it is detached
and not malicious. The disorder of the war is present, but it
is seen as from a distance, and passed over quickly. From the
beginning, the reader senses that Thomas is moving toward
death and he follows that swift movement rather than the
surrounding disorders of war. Truth, for Cocteau, in its
deepest sense, is in Thomas. The book is not about war, but
about the soul of Thomas where war is reflected in the importance of the young hero, in his dreams and exaltation and
in the dangers he welcomes as if they were poems to be read.

Cocteau's art makes the final scene inevitable and truth-
ful, when Thomas alone walks into a climate of war and is
shot. We realize that the bullet that pierces his heart is
the reality of life which will always defeat such a creature of
charm and fantasy. Thomas is one of the prodigal sons of
the twentieth century. He is the adolescent hero who incarnates the wisdom and the fate of adolescence. He continues the lineage of Augustin in Alain Fournier's *Le Grand
Meaulnes* (1913), and of Lafcadio in Gide's *Les Caves du
Vatican* (1914), and of Marcel in Proust's *Du Côté de chez
Swann* (1913). These three books, completed before the
outbreak of the war in 1914, are prolonged in the adolescent
hero Thomas who participates in the war and learns that the
world is ready to receive a youth so full of fantasies, so free

in his movements, so able to impose his imposture on the world of adults.

The adolescent hero, created by Jean Cocteau in the twenties in *Le Grand écart* and *Thomas l'imposteur* at the beginning of the decade soon after the war, and analyzed more fully in the two books at the end of the decade—the unsigned *Le Livre blanc* (1928) and *Les Enfants terribles* of 1929—is of a dangerous race, almost a race of privileged angels. This adolescent hero, created not only by Cocteau but by an adolescent century as well, lives by the belief that boldness and originality are forms of beauty to be exploited because the years of adolescence are brief. Life triumphs for the adolescent in his defiance of convention. The poetry of such a life is the upsetting of established values, but it is so brief, so swift that the disorder it brings is only temporary, only imaginary.

By their own lives Radiguet and Cocteau lived more closely to the heroes of *Thomas l'imposteur* and *Le Diable au corps* than most of the major writers of the first three decades who were attracted to the adolescent hero: Gide, in *Les Caves du Vatican* and *Les Faux-Monnayeurs*, Proust in *Du Côté de chez Swann* and *A l'ombre des jeunes filles en fleur*, Alain-Fournier in *Le Grand Meaulnes*, Montherlant in *Les Bestiaires*, Thomas Mann in *Blood of the Walsungs*, Aldous Huxley in *Point Counterpoint*.

Le Livre blanc, first published in 1928 without the author's name is a version of *Le Grand écart* and announces the theme of Dargelos, to be used a few months later in *Les Enfants terribles* and in *Le Sang d'un poète*. It is Cocteau's clearest statement on the tragic effect of beauty on those who appear to be the least affected by it. *Les privilèges de la beauté sont immenses. Elle agit même sur ceux qui paraissent s'en soucier le moins.*

The word *enfant terrible* has been lavishly applied to Cocteau himself. And even at the moment when he was received into the Académie Française, because there he seemed more than ever the *enfant terrible* in midst of the conservative solemn group of academicians. André Maurois' gracious word of welcome in his reception speech was his advice to Cocteau to remain Heurtebise, to remain *l'enfant terrible.* The word has come to designate not only Cocteau, not only the type of adolescent hero, but also a new type of creative spirit, one comparable to the *poète maudit* as defined by Verlaine a generation earlier. He is not unlike the *chassé,* the outlaw hunted by the police. He is often an *apatride,* a man without nationality.

In *Les Enfants terribles,* Cocteau gives to the already invented adolescent hero a new ardor and a new ingenuousness. The *enfants terribles* are almost mythic creatures endowed with some form of grace that permits them to defy conventions and all rational approaches to their problems. They are avid and curious, graceful and irreverent. With their beauty and the good fortune that presides over much of their lives, they make the adults around them seem like Pharisees. The action of their lives seems to be improvised. Even in their movements of ferociousness there is poetry. They are children whose pleasure comes not in playing with toys but in taking apart the toys in order to see what makes them work. In American literature they have their counterparts in the adolescent heroes of Salinger and Carson McCullers. More so than in Cocteau, they were incarnated in Raymond Radiguet, whose life bears a strange identity with a fictional *enfant terrible.*

He reappears in Dargelos, who throws the hard snowball in the opening scene of Cocteau's novel, and in Paul himself who is wounded by the snowball. The insolent formulas that Paul and Elisabeth hurl at one another are comparable to the snowballs fashioned by the ruthless Dargelos. Lafcadio, of *Les Caves du Vatican*, was this type of *enfant terrible*, who presided over the years between his appearance, in 1914, and approximately 1925. Paul, appearing at the end of the twenties, represents another type, a disillusioned *enfant terrible*, more introverted, more tragic. Early in the decade, the immediate life of action pursued by the adolescent hero was a liberation from a life of dogma and bourgeois morality. But late in the decade, the Dionysian way of life had grown into a deep-seated restlessness. The ubiquitous agile Lafcadio had become the immobilized youth sitting in one of the cosmopolitan bars, or Paul refusing to leave the suffocating atmosphere of his room.

Accused by his critics on countless occasions of creating "merely" fantasy characters in his books, characters that have no relationship with the seriousness of life, Cocteau today is being revindicated by readers who find in Dargelos of the novel, in Orphée of the film, in Heurtebise of the poem, examples of fictional characters who come from the deepest part of Cocteau's understanding of himself and of his period in history. It is increasingly clear that nothing in Cocteau's work is gratuitous or lacking in seriousness or merely eccentric. His fictional art is not a copy of reality, but the creation of a further reality. He imposes characters distinct from other fictional characters. Among themselves, Cocteau's heroes, Jacques Forestier, Thomas l'imposteur, and Paul l'enfant terrible bear resemblances, and a distant relationship with Orphée the assassinated poet.

While staying at a clinic in Saint-Cloud, in 1929, Jean Cocteau wrote a journal account of his recovery from his addiction to opium. The journal was later published under the title *Opium*. The idea of *Les Enfants terribles* occurred to him forcibly at this time in the clinic and he wrote the novel within the space of three weeks. It is based on school memories of la Cité Monthiers, of snowball fights, of the pupil Dargelos, of the story of a brother and sister. These were some of the ingredients from reality that went into the composition of this work that had an immediate success, and that has continued to the present time to interest a wide public, especially a youthful public. It is perhaps the most tragic expression that Cocteau ever gave to human destiny. Its success, during the decade following its publication, was such that the novel was compared, in terms of its effect on the public, to Goethe's *Werther*.

It is distinctly a novel about adolescence, about the action of destiny which draws a brother and sister toward a tragic end because they have a purity of spirit, because they refuse to alter the purity and the laws of adolescence. A dramatic tension never relaxes in the narrative from the beginning to the end. From the viewpoint of the adult world, the behavior of the brother and sister, Paul and Elisabeth, is inhuman throughout the story. They make no compromise with the society from which they are determined to live apart. They are bound together by symbolic games which are rites of a logic that is true only for them. Two outside friends are admitted to their tiny world, Gérard and Agathe, and their intermittent presence makes the actions and thoughts of Paul and Elisabeth appear more monstrous than ever. As long as the games can be played in the room they share together, their protective isolated world remains intact. Only when Elisabeth, the stronger of the two, realizes that Paul is attempting to leave the room and the games that had magically joined them does she kill her brother and take her own life.

The room, like the unity of place in a classical tragedy, is literally the world in which Paul and Elisabeth live. It is the setting of their lives and of their pact with destiny, their resolution not to compromise with the false world of adults. But it is also, in its compressed disorder, the picture of their inner life where they live in accordance with what Cocteau calls poetry. In *Les Enfants terribles* in particular, which is perhaps the clue to all the other works, poetry is an obscure force controlling the life of an individual, one of the mysterious names for death. With the very first scene of the novel, we are in the presence of death, and we never leave it, until death declares itself violently and blatantly in the final scene. At that moment, the room, which has served as a temporary beguiling tomb, takes off and moves into some vaster space far above the fixed site of tragedy.

At one point in the text the room is called a theatre whose performance begins at eleven in the evening: *le théâtre de la chambre ouvrait à 11 heures du soir*. It is exactly that: the setting of a play where Paul and his sister enact their roles and develop their characterizations. One is a spectator for the other, and when Gérard and Agathe are present in the room, Paul and Elisabeth are both actors who have a very real sense of performance. The first appearance of Dargelos initiates the action of the play. The snowball scene outside the school in the late afternoon when it is turning dark, is the prologue, after which the action continues for the most part in the lighted bedroom. At the end of the "play," the black ball of poison, sent by the invisible Dargelos, insti-

gates the tragic epilogue. The initial wound was deadly, and
the tragedy terminates when the time allotted runs out for
the two protagonists.

From the very beginning, when Paul, after the accident,
is brought into the room by Gérard, and Elisabeth mocks
both of them, but begins to take care of her brother, we
realize that the lives of the brother and sister have been so
joined, so conjugated one with the other, that they form one
destiny. This early scene prepares us for the dual suicide,
which is one suicide, at the end. Gérard watches them and
listens to them in bewilderment. He will remain the innocent, the bystander who understands nothing, but who
feels the strong attraction to the brother and sister which
is the attraction felt by readers of the novel, and the spectators of the film. He is hypnotized and has no real need of
understanding. Tragedy exerts on its spectators the power
of hypnosis and involves them within an action that is
both inexplicable and fatal. When Agathe comes into the
room in the early part of the novel, her resemblance to Dargelos forces us to suspect what actually does happen in the
outer aspect of the plot: Paul's attraction to her and finally
his love for her. This love is a solemn part of the rites of
adolescence. These rites were celebrated in the opening
snowball scene and at the end when Elisabeth wills her
brother's and her own death. The doors of the room are
closed forever. The tragic ending of adolescence is transcribed in the form of an apotheosis. The game of childhood
is finally played for keeps.

Between these two moments in Les Enfants terribles: the
prologue in which destiny announces itself in the celebration
of a love ritual (le collège célèbre ses sacrifices) and the
epilogue in which destiny concludes its action in the same
celebration of the same love, speechless and violent, we

watch Paul and Elisabeth enact a few scenes of their lives with the cold imperturbability of those who know instinctively that the moments granted to them for living are few and will soon be exhausted. They accept the fatal promiscuity of their room because they know it is all they will have in life. They are of another race and they refuse to expose themselves uselessly to the commonplace catastrophes of mankind.

Childhood demands a secret place. Children habitually construct some kind of retreat from the world, a site cut off from the impinging world of adults. The novelist shows us this place—the room of the brother and sister—and its fatal promiscuity. They live concealed from any family, from any city, from any historical period, and they behave in accord with the logic they improvise, as within a game. At first, Paul and Elisabeth are indifferent to the intruders Gérard and Agathe. Elisabeth's marriage to Mikhael was only a brief episode—one has the premonition of its brevity from the beginning—and on Mikhael's death, the room is reconstructed. Elisabeth had never interrupted the spell of childhood, she had simply annexed Mikhael as a subsidiary game. But when she realizes that Paul's love for Agathe means the end of the enchantment, she undertakes to perform the one act that will terminate childhood and the reign of the room. Anything else would be a compromise, a way of permitting the spell of childhood slowly to change, slowly to fuse with the logic of adult make-believe.

The beauty of *Les Enfants terribles* is oracular. Elisabeth held longer than Paul the dreams of childhood; she cherished longer than her brother did the perfect happiness of childhood games. And this permits her, at the end of the novel, to become the great actress, alone in the house, convinced of a supernatural mission, as she mounts and descends the stairway. She is the sister who has now truly become Electra, the preserver of values, whose greatness is enhanced by the absolutism of the act she commits. She defies everyone and everything. *Seule contre tous avec la chambre, elle bravait Agathe, elle bravait Gérard, elle bravait Paul, elle bravait le monde entier.* Her characterization is both that of a child and a criminal. Each one of these parts cancels out the other, and she finally appears as a goddess presiding over the destiny of her brother, infallible and inhuman. She is the figure of death, cohabiting with Paul, until the time comes for her to take over her brother and convert a life story into a fable. The ending of the book is an assumption. The brother and sister rise up through space to become a constellation, and even the room is released from its bondage as if it were a balloon. The earth and the pitiable cries of the human race are left so far below that they become indistinct and indistinguishable in space and time.

The writing of *Les Enfants terribles* is such that at no one point in the narrative is the imagination of the reader restricted. As he reads, he creates another world beside the story of Paul and Elisabeth. It is a world to accompany and explain theirs. The economy of the writing is such that another spiritual order is necessary for the reader, in order to accept the bareness and the coldness of the written story. The text of Cocteau needs an illumination from outside, from the reader's knowledge of mankind and mythological heroes, from his knowledge of city apartments and supernatural forces that control and explain human destiny. The tensed bareness of Cocteau's style in *Les Enfants terribles* comes from the agility with which he moves back and forth between the concentrated promiscuity of the room where two lives are so joined that they really make one life, and the limitless freedom of the spirit, which is the imagination of childhood that needs only a few talismans kept in a drawer to create an existence without bonds and obligations.

Les Enfants terribles is the first full study of the theme of fate in the work of Cocteau. It is never totally absent from his earlier works, and it will be deepened in the film of 1932, *Le Sang d'un poète,* and in the play of 1934, *La Machine infernale.* All three works are illustrations of the familiar romantic thesis that the poet writes with his blood. The snowball and the black balls of poison, the fetichistic objects kept in the drawer of the children's room, and the room itself are used magically to convey the idea of the life controlled by invisible forces. This use of *trucages* (tricks) will be everywhere in *Le Sang d'un poète,* and in the myth of Oedipus of *La Machine infernale.* The esoteric is a somewhat disguised ingredient in this novel, but it becomes obvious in the black ball of poison at the end by means of which all the themes are fused into the one theme of timed fatality.

The art of the film and the art of the stage are purely the arts of illusion where Cocteau is justified in experimenting with the problem of illusion and reality. But Paul in the novel, as well as the poet in the film, and Oedipe in the play, are all prototypes of the searcher, of the man looking for the truth behind the lie or the illusion. Whether it be in a snowball, or a statue, or a scarred foot, Cocteau's hero is the youth eager to read his destiny, to piece together the meagre events of his life in order to understand his life and see it on the walls of a room or in the lines of a soothsayer. *Les Enfants terribles* is the first major effort of Cocteau to answer the harassing question: how far can a man know his destiny? how can he know himself? The female figure in *La Machine infernale* is the sphinx destined to undo men one after the other. In *Le Sang d'un poète* the statue of a woman is in the poet's room and speaks cryptic sentences destined to warn and predict. In *Les Enfants terribles*, Elisabeth is first the sister of Paul, but she becomes by the end of the novel a sphinx-like goddess who has the power to condemn and slay in order to preserve in her own mysterious way the charmed life of the hero who has been assigned to her for questions about the reason for life and the fatality of death.

VI
THE POET
AS DRAMATIST

THE HISTORY of Cocteau's theatre illustrates more clearly than other aspects of his work his belief that the new in art is necessary, that the artist is the man who opposes what is currently fashionable. The authentic artist counterbalances. He will often upset the traditional. *Parade*, Cocteau's first work for the stage, was in direct contrast to the naturalist theatre of the day. Years later, when Cocteau's experimental writing for the theatre had been more accepted and when it had in fact created its own posterity and disciples, he returned to traditional forms, as in *L'Aigle à deux têtes*, strongly reminiscent of the romantic melodrama. What has often been falsely called a tendency toward insolence in Cocteau's writings, is closer to a deeply-felt need for novelty, for contrast.

The bizarre concoctions of the earliest Cocteau: *Le Boeuf sur le toit*, of 1920, and *Les Mariés de la Tour Eiffel*, of 1921, were efforts to reanimate the French theatre that did appear lifeless during the year following the First World War. By its nature, the art of the theatre has to be a constant renova-

57

tion, a constant experimentation. The public quickly tires of the familiar formulas. Cocteau embraced the theatre as an art which would permit him a startling use of magic and the unusual (*l'insolite*). Never in agreement with his own time, Cocteau created his own fashions, his own genres. But his tireless search for the new was never an expression of animosity for what was currently in favor. Cocteau is an inventor. He proposes something new, but it is not in the form of an attack. For more than thirty years, between *Parade* of 1917 and *Bacchus* of 1951, Jean Cocteau was associated with the theatre in Paris, and each work was the proposal of something new.

The theatre is the art of illusion. What we see on the stage is a lie not in the moral sense, but in the philosophical sense of appearance as opposed to reality, and in the aesthetic sense of fiction as opposed to history. This profound lesson of the theatre never ceased to hold and fascinate Cocteau. The actors in costume played parts, not themselves. This was a new sincerity, that of the role; a new activity, that of ceremony. As the actors performed, a personality was created on the stage which was the creation of the dramatist. An adventure was simulated, and the spectators believed in the simulation, and the spectators believed in the simulation as long as it lasted. The spot lights revealed another world, a luminous world larger and clearer than life.

As if it were a charm destined to form and justify his life, Jean Cocteau underwent the experience of the theatre in all of its aspects: words devised by the dramatist, make-up on the faces of the actors, a public watching for two hours the enactment of pathos, of human frailty, of farcical behavior, of catastrophe. A place where all of this is projected by deception and tricks of light, sound, space, and action; where no one is oneself, not even the spectators because they too turn into intriguers as they watch.

On the stage, life becomes interpretation of life. The dramatic poet is an illusionist who makes us believe we are
watching Phèdre's jealousy, or Hamlet's madness. Cocteau
accepted easily all the rules of the theatre, as if they had been
created for him: the effort to give to fiction a sense of truth,
and the effort to find for an actor a new personality. His protagonists are men in search of their destinies, in search of the
meaning of their lives. They are usually men who understand
themselves imperfectly and who find, during the course of
the action, someone to answer their questions, to offer them
some explanation of the drama in which they find themselves
involved. Orphée is helped by the female figure of Death and
by Angel Heurtebise, incarnated as a window-repairer. The
Sphinx, as a young girl, explains the enigma to Oedipe.

In the plays of Cocteau there is nothing comparable to
Claudel's faith which permeates the works of the Catholic
dramatist. There is nothing as permanent as the theme of
protest in the plays of Jean Anouilh. And there is no phi-
losophy as clearly indicated as in the existentialist plays of
Jean-Paul Sartre. There is no trace of what might be called
a message. By comparison with such playwrights, Cocteau's
art is gratuitous, it is purely the art of the theatre. It is the
enactment of enigmas, magic, incantation, as in the sphinx
scene of *La Machine Infernale*, and the alphabet scene of
Orphée. It is the dramatization of various forms of fate that
subdue and imprison the human will. The word itself, *machine*, used twice in the title of Cocteau's plays, implies the
ingeniousness of the gods in trapping men, in making them
into pathetic and helpless beings.

For the subject matter of his plays, Cocteau borrows
abundantly from other dramatists, from mythology and history, but he gives to the borrowed theme a new swiftness,
a tempo more in keeping with the jumbled precipitation of
the twentieth century. His *Antigone*, for example, is a reduc-

tion of the Sophocles' text, with a single figure representing the chorus and with Antigone's farewell speech to Thebes resembling an aria. With each of his plays, Cocteau renovates some aspect of the theatrical art. He is instinctively a man of the theatre who is caught by the spell of the stage, by the lighting and the set as well as by the tense atmosphere in the wings, and who is also fully conscious of the perpetual risk of the theatre. He knows that each performance is a privileged moment that will be over with the final curtain, but that has the chance the following night to form again and cast another spell with the same brevity that characterizes danger.

Parade, of 1917, does not have the importance of a text. It is important in the sense of being a collaboration between Cocteau and Picasso, when the poet learned from the painter certain lessons that were to guide him thereafter. A sense of clairvoyance, first. Not clarity, but an illumination coming from the inner life of the spirit, a unity of spirit presiding over a strange assembly of beings and objects. This first art of Cocteau was quite in keeping with the new graphic art that was beginning to come from the *ateliers* of Montparnasse and Montmartre. *Parade* was one example of the graphic metamorphosis initiated by cubism and which was to be continued by surrealism. From the experiment of *Parade*, Cocteau learned also that inspiration must not protrude from the final work. Art must be a collaboration between a seriousness of theme and a lightness of form which is almost a disguise of the theme. This theory is in Cocteau's sentence describing Picasso's art: *Arlequin habite Port-Royal*.

Picasso was responsible for the sets, costumes, and props of *Parade* and Cocteau was responsible for the story, the characters, and the choreography. Choreographic notes replaced a text in *Parade*. The characters might have come from a music hall sketch: a Chinese prestidigitator, an American girl, acrobats, managers, a languorous horse. There were noises of dynamos, boat sirens, typewriters, and airplanes. There was pantomime, dancing, and music.

Le Boeuf sur le toit (1920) was also a mime performed by the Fratellini clowns, with music by Darius Milhaud and a set by Raoul Dufy. With *Les Mariés de la Tour Eiffel* of 1921, the genre was an amalgam of play, pantomime, and dance. The text was spoken by two actors disguised as phonographs. Cocteau's preface to the published text is a manifesto calling for a new poetic theatre in which the poet's role is the discovery of the meaning of familiar objects surrounding him. The poet writing for the theatre should rehabilitate the commonplace and substitute a poetic play for poetry in the theatre. Music for *Les Mariés* was provided by five composers from the group of *Les Six*: Auric, Milhaud, Poulenc, Honegger, and Taillefer. The marriage party was a picture of the familiar daily world.

In Greek mythology, Orpheus is the founder of the Orphic mysteries and the creator of the myth of Dionysos, the god who was dismembered and then resuscitated. Dionysos symbolizes the frenzy of living, the genius of individuality, the animation of nature in its multiple forms. Apollo, his brother, is the god of inspiration and of eternal beauty who presides over the spiritual world. Dionysos presides over the world of matter. But the two brothers are not enemies. They work together. They are both necessary. Apollo is the god of the Muses, and Dionysos the god of the Bacchantes. Orpheus, in his life and in his works, joins the two divinities: Apollo and Dionysos, man and woman, priest and bacchante, sun and moon. Orpheus gives expression to thoughts that are

Apollonian and experiences Dionysian enthusiasm. When his wife Eurydice dies, he descends to hell where the infernal spirits give Eurydice back to him on the condition that he will not look at her as they are leaving hell. He does look, and loses her forever. Then his limbs are torn from his body by the Bacchantes.

Cocteau's first original play of some importance was *Orphée*, written in 1925. The time of the action is today as well as an imaginary Thrace. Orphée is the national poet of his country. He has brought home a mysterious horse (the winged horse Pegasus was once the symbol of poetic inspiration) that dictates to him by means of a ouija-board an incomprehensible sentence: *Madame Eurydice reviendra des enfers.* Eurydice is in love with her husband. When she married Orphée, she left the club of the Bacchantes, presided over by Aglaonice who, furious with Eurydice, prophesied disaster.

When the play opens, it is obvious that the horse has bewitched Orpheus. He attaches great improtance to the slightest words given by the horse, and Eurydice is shocked and saddened by her husband's behavior. She confides in a mysterious window-glass repairer called Heurtebise, who has the habit of calling on Eurydice each day. In reality, Heurtebise is an angel who is watching over the destiny of Orphée and Eurydice.

(One day when he was calling on Picasso, at his studio on the rue de la Boétie, Cocteau heard a voice say to him in the elevator: "My name is on the plate." He read on the brass plate of the control lever: *Ascenseur Heurtebise.* Heurtebise became the angel of his poem and the angel in *Orphée.*)

Aglaonice succeeds in poisoning Eurydice who, before she dies, pleads with Heurtebise to bring Orphée back from his enchantment. Death, as a beautiful woman, takes Eurydice into the realm of Death. Orphée does lose Eurydice by looking at her, and is torn asunder by the Bacchantes. The last scene, in heaven, shows us the couple reunited.

Death, in Cocteau's play, is represented as an elegantly dressed woman, because most people imagine her in the form of a skeleton. Mirrors are gateways to death for Cocteau because, if we look at ourselves in a mirror, we can see death working there as bees work in a glass hive. When Heurtebise points to the mirror as the way Orphée should take in order to find Eurydice, he explains that mirrors are related to windows:

> *Heurtebise*: Voilà votre route.
> *Orphée*: Où avez-vous appris?
> *Heurtebise*: Les Miroirs? Ça rentre dans la vitre.

The play is the drama of poetry, the drama of those possessed by poetry. It is on the relationship between an artist and his inspiration. This inspiration is sometimes called his genius or his personal demon, which in this case is represented by the horse. When Orphée says at the beginning of the play that the horse enters his night and brings back sentences from there *(Ce cheval entre dans ma nuit. Il en rapporte des phrases. . . .)* we realize that the horse is the hidden subconscious of the poet. Every part of the play's action is a commentary on the mystery of poetic creation. At times, Eurydice is the public when she fails to understand why the official poet gives up his official position for a horse. The demands of a poetic work are incompatible with a normal life. Eurydice is hurt by what she considers neglect. She is shocked also by Heurtebise when she observes something supernatural in his behavior. *Je vous croyais simple,* she says to him. *Je vous croyais de ma race, vous êtes de celle du cheval.*

When the sentence dictated by the horse is first articulated at the beginning of the play, it sounds absurd. But it turns out to be literally true. In accepting the mysterious message, Orphée accepts his destiny. The secrecy of the poet's fate is humorously depicted in the scene with the police commissioner at the end of the play. The *commissaire* mistakes Heurtebise for a tramp and is puzzled by all the traces of the supernatural in this drama of poetry and death. The opening scene of the quarrel between Orphée and Eurydice might easily be a musical comedy sketch; the scene in which Death operates on Eurydice might come from a mystery melodrama; the sacrifice of Orphée when he accepts his fate (*la vie me taille, Heurtebise*) is a tragic scene; and the commissioner's scene at the end is burlesque. The coherence of the play is the language by which all aspects of the story are translated into theatrical images. The poetic conception of Orphée forces the spectators to accept a prophesying horse, an angelic window-repairer, and Death in the form of a lady wearing an evening dress.

Orphée contains no symbols. The supernatural is treated as if it were real. Since it was first performed by the Pitoeffs in 1926, it has been played countless times in university theatres throughout the world. Rainer Maria Rilke was so moved by Reinhardt's production in Berlin in 1927 that he sent a congratulatory message to Cocteau in which he said that the myth was revealed to the French poet, who returned from it, his skin tanned as from the seashore. *Dites à Jean Cocteau que je l'aime, lui seul à qui s'ouvre le mythe dont il revient hâlé comme du bord de la mer.*

Whenever Cocteau chooses for a play a legend from antiquity, he interprets and rejuvenates it. Sophocles' version of the Oedipus story emphasizes the fate of a noble family.

Oedipus, son of Laius, is induced to kill his father, whom he did not recognize; to guess the riddle of the sphinx; and to marry his mother, whom he did not recognize. The revelation of his crimes moves him to blind himself and go into exile. On this subject matter Cocteau invents modern variations and allusions to our age.

In the first act of *La Machine infernale*, obviously inspired by the opening scene of *Hamlet*, soldiers are speaking on the ramparts of Thebes and waiting for the appearance of the ghost of the slain king. In spite of the soothsayer Tiresias, who knows what infernal machine the gods will set in motion when humans try to see too clearly, Jocasta insists upon seeing her husband's ghost. But the ghost, who is trying to warn his people of the woes to come, cannot be heard.

In the second act, young Oedipus, who has just slain his father, comes into the presence of the sphinx. He knows that the one who conquers the sphinx will marry Jocasta and become king. The sphinx is in the form of a young girl who is weary of killing for the god Anubis and tries to make herself attractive to Oedipus. She reveals to him the secret of the riddle and thus allows him to slay her.

The third act is the marriage night, a bedroom scene of sinister forebodings. At every moment the mother and son, who do not know one another, almost come upon the truth of the situation, but a tragic ambiguity prevents this. The will of the gods keeps them within their blindness.

Seventeen years lapse between acts three and four. In accordance with the traditional legend, Oedipe discovers that he is the murderer of his father and the husband of his mother. In this act Cocteau closely follows Sophocles: Jocaste hangs herself, Oedipe gouges out his eyes, Antigone will accompany her father and lead him into exile.

A scene from the 1954 production of *La Machine infernale*, staged in Paris with Jean Marais as Oedipus and Jeanne Moreau as the Sphinx

The text of the play was written in 1932 and given its first performance in April 1934, an important date in Cocteau's career because it initiated that part of his career as a successful playwright when he reached a fairly wide and enthusiastic audience. The earlier run of *Orphée*, put on by the Pitoeffs, had lasted only a few nights. *La Voix humaine* had been performed at the Comédie-Française, but it was a single act, with one character. Jouvet had accepted the text and was to put it on in his theatre of La Comédie-des-Champs-Elysées, and had scheduled the première for April. It was one of the fashionable theatres of the day, with Dullin's Atelier in Montmartre.

In January, Cocteau had been thinking of Jean-Pierre Aumont for the part of Oedipe. Aumont had already played the lead in a film: *Le Lac aux Dames*, and continued to play small parts in Jouvet's company. He was surprised when Cocteau sent for him to come to his apartment on the rue Vignon. As soon as he entered Cocteau's room, the writer said to him: "You will play Oedipe" *(Vous serez mon Oedipe)*. Aumont, who knew that Jouvet was considering Charles Boyer and Pierre Blanchard for the role of Oedipe, blurted out: "But you don't know me." The answer was the same. *"Vous serez mon Oedipe.* Forget you know Jean-Pierre. Look at him differently. He is Oedipe."

Rehearsals began in February. Cocteau had hoped to have Elvire Popesco as Jocaste, but she was engaged, and the part was taken by Marthe Régnier. (Twenty years later, Elvire Popesco did play Jocaste in the important revival with Jean Marais.) There were three months of rehearsals and eighty performances in 1934. Jouvet was as always a demanding, difficult director. Jean-Pierre Aumont has described his own entrance in the second act, as he walked down an inclined plateau with a mercurial light on him and came abruptly

face to face with the sphinx. Christian Bérard, the set designer, had strewn bones over Oedipe's entrance, the remains of the victims of the sphinx. Before the curtain each
evening Aumont made a path for himself among the bones,
for fear of stumbling, and each evening Bérard put them
back into place, just before the curtain went up.

Cocteau was often backstage in the dressing rooms of the
actors and carried on with them long discussions about the
play and the performances and the reactions of the public.
He used to say that he had not written a line of the play,
that the text had been dictated to him one night, and it
formed one unit, so mysteriously compact, that not one
line could be changed. He proclaimed the paradox that a
playwright composes one play, the actors perform another,
and the public hears a third. Every theatrical success is a
misunderstanding.

Cocteau became obsessed with the conviction that only
the younger members of the audience liked the play, that
only a thousand people had seen *La Machine infernale*, and
they were the same ones who came back each night to the
theatre. The play did create its fanatics, and there were fights
among the students in the audience which recalled the performances of *Hernani*, one hundred years earlier.

In the revival of *La Machine infernale* of 1954 Jeanne
Moreau played the sphinx and gave to the famous monologue
in Act II a *brio* that made the performance memorable. For
Act III the setting resembled a cage for the nuptial scene
between Queen Jocaste and Oedipe. It is the moment when,
in Cocteau's dramaturgy, destiny offers the royal couple a few
hints of tragedy. The audience realizes this rather than the
victims. Elvire Popesco, as Jocaste, wept over the wounded
feet of Oedipe, and spoke in a strong foreign accent, and
confused masculine and feminine genders. Jean Marais ap-

peared almost as a Greek hero and used in his diction a peculiarity he had developed in his career, that of accenting the first syllable of important words. The two figures in Act III seemed to be caught in their royal mantles. The setting of Christian Bérard, the tension of the actors, the signs of disaster in the text, and even the diction of the queen and her son, made of this act a dramatic triumph. Twenty years had been necessary to make of the play a classic. The long speech of the sphinx was respected, and the novelties that Cocteau added to the legend were admired: the sphinx as a young girl falling in love with Oedipe, the marriage-night scene, the apparition of Jocaste at the end to guide Oedipe toward his destiny.

The "machine" is a timed machine, the hours of his illusions, which, when they are exhausted, destroy man with the suddenness of a machine stopped. The image represents a theological surveillance over a human life.

In the fourth act, Oedipe is the gambler who knows that he has lost. When he sets out accompanied by members of his family, forming almost a group of Pirandello characters, the spectators realize that the legend of Oedipe is beginning, that a mythical journey is going to lead him beyond life. However, throughout the first three acts, a sense of modern life is very much in the foreground. The machine is behind everything, and the machine is true reality, carefully concealed in the dark. But the conversation of the soldiers in the first act, heard against jazz music coming from the cafés below, might almost refer to the Berlin Wall or Vietnam. Jocaste is a matron from today's society and Oedipe a young athlete. He illustrates what Freud has taught our world: that the birth trauma, the birth anxiety may be quelled in a man when he returns to his mother and makes of her an object of sexual pleasure.

The third act is essentially a scene of sleeping wherein Oedipe relives the anxiety of his birth. Only incest will calm the anxiety. The sphinx, encountered in the second act, was a premonitory symbol of the mother, in her character of strangler, in the threat she represents. And Oedipe, in conquering the sphinx, in Cocteau's version, overcomes the first wave of anxiety in his life. The entire scene with Cocteau's sphinx is the traumatic drama of birth as analyzed by Freud. When at the end of the act, Oedipe throws the body of the sphinx over his shoulder, he resembles the dancer in the rite of Dionysos. The skin of the goat or the ram is the once protective womb of the mother, which has now lost its usefulness. The role of the sphinx to which Cocteau gives such importance in *La Machine infernale* is ambiguous because as a young girl, she tries to turn Oedipe away from incest (*épouse une femme plus jeune que toi*), but at the same time she leads him to his fate, to his Nemesis.

With his play of 1937, *Les Chevaliers de la table ronde*, Cocteau declared he had broken his infatuation with Greece, but in reality he had simply moved from one myth to another. The fundamental preoccupation is the same in *La Machine infernale* and *Les Chevaliers*, which is that of the tragic writer, the implacable logic he sees in the all-powerful forces that control the destiny of men. Whatever transpires in his plays in terms of dramatic action is in terms of the absolute. He is in this sense one of the most traditionally tragic writers of modern France. In commenting on his own plays, he has often used the word *supplice*, and warns the spectators that they are going to watch not a spectacle in the usual sense, but a scene of torture.

In choosing the medieval subject of the knights of the round table, he was actually choosing a theme closely related to the story of Electra. When the hero Galaad repeats over and over that it is necessary to pay up for what has happened: *il faut payer, payer, payer,* he is stating the law of Cocteau's dramaturgy, which is also the law of ancient Greek tragedy. In a superficial sense, the air of mysteriousness in *Les Chevaliers de la table ronde* is medieval, or reminiscent of the medieval. But he is profoundly concerned as a dramatist with the final moment, when, in the bursting of an explosion, the secret of men and the secret of things are supernaturally (or magically) revealed.

The elaborate scenic surprises and mystifications called for in the text are not absolutely necessary, because the enchantment is in the action. It does not depend on flashes of lightning and claps of thunder. The castle of Camelot is intoxicated and drugged by a network of lies. Merlin's power derives from the power of deceit. Evil presides over the castle, in the adultery which is concealed and in the acts of betrayal which are disguised. When Galaad the pure knight appears, the evil spell is broken: the sun comes into view, the grass begins again to grow, and the birds sing. The Grail that had been lost is recovered by the white-armored knight. But the revelation of truth brings punishment and death. King Arthur slays his wife and the treacherous knight.

Les Chevaliers de la table ronde is a continuation of Cocteau's oracular tradition in the theatre, so apparent in *Orphée, Antigone,* and *La Machine infernale.* The first act shows the castle under the spell of evil, and the inhabitants either accepting it or in revolt against it. Galaad (Parsifal) arrives and breaks the spell by projecting disorder into the lives of those who accept the spell. Act II reveals the source of the evil: Merlin the magician and his slave the demon Ginifer who can be transformed into any character. The occult force in Galaad is now set up against the occult force in Merlin. Act III is the disenchantment of the castle. With the restoration of truth, Galaad prepares to leave. The law of the poet-knight demands that he not stay where he is loved. The play is over with the king's recovery, and the newly-restored health of the land.

Les Chevaliers is the most prodigal of Cocteau's plays, the richest in diversity. Its subject, drawn from French medieval legends (as are *Renaud et Armide, L'Eternel retour,* and *La Belle et la bête*) is, in its deepest sense, the struggle between truth and falsehood being waged in a man's heart. In the recovery of truth at the end of the play, King Arthur suffers the most and Galaad warns him that everything will be difficult, that truth is painful at first. As he looks at the slain bodies of Lancelot and the queen, he declares his preference for real corpses over a false life: *J'aime mieux de vrais morts qu'une fausse vie.*

The demon Ginifer, as slave of Merlin, is invisible and appears only in the forms of Gauvain, the queen, and Galaad. These three characters are at times true and at other times false, and these incarnations of Ginifer provide the burlesque scenes of the play. Ginifer is Cocteau's dramatic invention. His treatment of Arthur's suffering is also an innovation. It increases steadily as a feverish malady throughout the play, and breaks out into a tragic ending. His hallucinations are made real for the spectators because they hear what he hears: the love dialogue between Lancelot and the queen.

After bringing up his public on Greek and medieval themes, Cocteau presented them with a melodrama, *Les Parents terribles* (1937), with Parisian characters dressed like Parisians of today. Disorder prevails in the Paris apartment. The mother Yvonne spends her life in a dressing gown, between her unmade bed and her bathroom. Her love for her son has exiled her from everything else in life. Her husband is a mild, flabby inventor whose inventions have not enriched him. His sister-in-law is an Electra, with the passion for bringing order to everything. Unmarried, she lives with the family and helps it in every way. These three characters are upset at the beginning of the play over the son's absence. When Michel does come, he is eager to announce his engagement to a charming girl, who is a book binder. Yvonne explodes with jealousy. The scene is violent, especially because the girl accepts the attention and financial help of another man. It turns out that Michel's father, Georges, is his rival, and that Electra-Léo, his sister-in-law, lends him the money he gives to Madeleine.

The second act is the meeting of the family with Madeleine. Her protector insists that she invent the existence of another lover, a younger one, in order to break off the marriage with Michel. Michel's despair fills most of Act III, and it is of such magnitude that the family agrees to permit the marriage. Yvonne commits suicide and order is restored with two marriages in view: Michel and Madeleine, and Georges and Léo who has been in love with Georges for twenty years.

The film of *Les Parents terribles* (1948) is practically the same work as the play. The text is the same and the actors are the same as those who created the parts (Jean Marais as Michel, Gabrielle Dorziat as Léo, Yvonne de Bray as Yvonne). The art of the camera makes them more human within the walls of the small apartment. *La roulotte* (gypsy wagon), as the apartment is called, is the confined space suitable for the three unities, and the camera does not focus on any outside landscape. In the theatre one is always aware of the wings on either side of the stage, but in the film the city is outside the apartment, unseen and containing the life of the city. There is no time for anything outside the intense concentrated action of the play. The time it takes for the performance coincides exactly with the time of the action. When all is over, *la roulotte* becomes a real Gypsy wagon, and it rumbles off with a tinkling of bells. Poignantly, Jean Cocteau's voice speaks to it.

In the guise of a boulevard melodrama, *Les Parents terribles* has affiliations with the Greek world of order and disorder. The figure of the mother, in her willful childishness, in the anarchy she portrays, is Antigone. Tante Léo and the young girl Madeleine are representatives of social order and they together bear the responsibilities of Creon. The boy Michel, hovering midway between the anarchic spirit of his mother and the social order of his aunt and fiancée, is the involuntary murderer, not of his father Laius, but of his mother Jocaste.

La Machine à écrire, written in 1941, was according to Cocteau's own harsh judgment a "disaster." But the first two acts are so well constructed that the weakness of the third act can be forgiven. The plot is complicated, and based upon the theory that the main problem in playwriting is to create a misunderstanding. A small provincial town is upset by a flood of anonymous letters. A police inspector has come from Paris to find the guilty person. In the home of the inspector's friend Didier, three members of the family claim to be the writer of the anonymous letters. Cocteau gives a picture of French provincial life just before the collapse of France in 1941, with its hypocritical attitudes and vices. Yet the interest in the play centers about the discovery of the guilty person.

Cocteau exploits the intrigue by depicting every character in the play as engaged in some kind of imposture. By indolence or by vanity they construct patterns of deceit. The play becomes the unmasking of the fundamental personality of the characters. The structure is so imposing, so involved, that the play is not able to sustain it. The complexity comes from the mythomanic actions of the young people, Maxime and Margot, who do not cease pretending to others and to themselves. In their behavior, it is never clear what is true and what is false. It is never clear where imagination ends and where reality begins.

L'Aigle à deux têtes, the Cocteau play most reminiscent of Hugo's melodrama, was only a partial success. It is an intelligent but far too cerebral attempt at playwriting, a virtuoso piece which seems more the vehicle for an actress than a play capable of holding audiences in successive generations. There are scenes of pure theatricality, such as the encounter of the queen with the intruder, the young revolutionary resembling her dead husband.

In the writing of this play which was obviously destined for the large theatre-going public, Cocteau omitted all elements that might have seemed strange or disconcerting or obscure. L'Aigle à deux têtes is a love drama, with extreme and violent peripeteia. It is almost the story of Ruy Blas, of a tragic love between a queen and a man of the people, of a conflict between love and the powers of the state. The queen's husband has been killed by a terrorist on the very day of their marriage. Since then, she has lived alone. In the first act she is about to begin another evening with the ghost of her husband, when shots are fired and a wounded man comes in through the window. He resembles the dead king. He is an anarchist who had come to kill the queen. What happens is inevitable: the queen falls in love with the anachist, whom she hides in the castle, and the young anarchist will not kill his queen but falls in love with her. Cocteau has written, as he said himself, "the story of an anarchist queen and an anarchist with a royal soul." The established order of the court prevents a revolution that would have assured the happiness of the couple. The young man poisons himself and with this action the final and most striking scene of the play begins. The queen feigns scorn and hatred of her lover until he stabs her. This is what she wanted. As they die, she tells him that she had lied.

Edwige Feuillère, who created the part of the queen, brought out the passion and pathos of this final scene. The synchronization of the two deaths on the stage of the Hébertot Theatre was impeccably conceived and carried out by Mme Feuillère and Jean Marais. And they repeated their triumph in the film version where the text, especially in the final scene, remained substantially the same.

The opening scene, at night, with its storm, the young queen alone, the sudden appearance at the window of a man who seems to be the king's ghost, are all elements of a romantic melodrama. The first act is a monologue of the queen. Stanislas, when he enters the room, refuses to answer her. She is a mythomaniac, who makes a tragedy out of her life and enacts this tragedy even when she is alone. The second act belongs to Stanislas who passionately unmasks the queen and reveals her pride and her play-acting. His violence in the second act is an answer to the queen's histrionics in the first act. The third act is the intervention of destiny. The final scene in which the queen plays the part of an enraged woman is the full portrait of the heroine. She is the actress, the *monstre sacré*, who convincingly pretends to be scornful and hateful.

Cocteau had announced *Bacchus*, first performed in December 1951, as a thesis play, but actually it is not that. It turned out to be the continuation of *Les Enfants terribles*. The three characters: the brother, the sister, and friend live in the sixteenth century, at the time of Luther, in a small German city. At this time, the friend—Hans—has the leading part. The sister becomes the mistress of Hans after refusing his advances. In the seduction, the girl seduced is in love with the seducer. And at the end, the brother kills Hans in order to spare him the horror of the stake or the shame of retribution.

Each year an inhabitant of the town is elected "Bacchus" and given full royal powers for a week. This time, the town simpleton is elected. This Hans, however, has simulated his idiocy. Once in power, he announces that he will build in one week the ideal city. The plans he makes are vaguely reminiscent of Rousseau's *Contrat social*. But the play is more concerned with the revolutionist than with the revolution. The adversary of Hans-Rousseau is a cardinal who, like Voltaire, has scathing wit and is secretly without faith. The old Rousseau-Voltaire controversy is merely one episode in the eternal quarrel between the young and the old, between idealists and rationalists. The second act is largely given over to the debate between Hans and the cardinal. It is more a debate between two temperaments than between two systems. The gentleness of the cardinal has a terrifying quality about it, and his intelligence, too, is awesome. In the debate, the *enfants terribles* lose to those in authority. Even the poor are in league with the rich, and at the end of the week, the crowd is waiting to seize Hans and burn him.

Bacchus is by no means one of the major texts of Cocteau. The first act is stilted and weak, the preaching throughout the play is excessive, the changes of heart in some of the characters are unexplained. At no point do the spectators imagine that Hans will win out; if this had been the case, it would have been highly dramatic. Blasphemy is not easy to make real and sustain. Hans has neither hate nor enough love to make his curse efficacious.

The quarrel that ensued between Mauriac and Cocteau over *Bacchus* seems today important only as an episode in the career of the playwright. It flared up a few days after the opening performance of *Bacchus*, when in a letter Mauriac published in *Le Figaro Littéraire* on December 29, 1951, he denounced the play as an attack on the Church. Whereas other critics pointed out the verboseness of the play, Mauriac seemed to be alone in his worry over the anti-religious implications. It is a play of ideas where two truths are opposed. Hans is the pure anarchist without a sense of order and strategy. The cardinal demonstrates the dangers of anarchy and points out the contradictions in Hans' arguments. The tragedy at the end is the solitude of the genius as he faces the crowd that has turned against him. The cardinal was right, because outside, the stake and the punishment are being prepared. It is both a fatal and a willed death. The hero gives the orders until the moment when the power which he himself has liberated, takes over and controls him.

In recent years, certain critics, and notably Pierre Dubourg, have attempted to give an essentially philosophical interpretation to Cocteau's plays and have resented the use of such a word as *jongleur* as applied to Cocteau in his capacity of dramatist. But the term *jongleur* does not necessarily have a pejorative connotaton. It refers to the apparent facility of Cocteau's writing, to the wit and ballet-like quality of many of the scenes. It would be unwise to deny these qualities that make up a large part of Cocteau's originality and style. In *Orphée*, tragedy is very much allied with the burlesque in the characters of the horse and Angel Heurtebise. An explanation, in philosophical terms, of the devices used by Cocteau in his dramaturgy tends to weaken their charm. This "charm" is precisely a spell which guards the seccret of beings and things. Poetry is a mystery for Cocteau and not a demonstration. Heurtebise and mirrors do not lend themselves easily to a traditional analysis.

Cocteau mimics so easily and transforms so well that one forgets he owes more to his immediate predecessors in the little theatre movement (or the poetic theatre) than to Sophocles. The dramatic innovations of Jarry and Apollinaire are used by him. The wit of his insights, the flash of his metaphors, the fluency of his style carry the best of his scenes. He uses what is at hand and mixes disparate, contradictory elements. The play *Orphée* is a recasting of the Greek myth, but it is also Cocteau's conversion to Catholicism, announced in the guardian angel Heurtebise, a nod of recognition to Jacques Maritain. The angel is a glazier, and in his *Lettre*, he calls Maritain a creature of glass.

VII
THE POET
IN HIS ART

Cocteau used the word "poetry" to designate all of his work: poetry of the novel, poetry of the theatre, poetry of criticism, of graphic art, of the cinema. And there are finally the several volumes for which the word poetry will have to stand alone. This part of his work is the least well known. It is neglected always for the other forms in which the poetic *elements* are important. Lines from the poems often reappear transformed in other works where they are given a more dramatic, more hallucinatory form. In *Plain-Chant*, for example, of 1923, death is described as not killing but having her assassins:

> Car ce n'est pas la mort elle-même qui tue.
> Elle a ses assassins.

Twenty-seven years later, in the film *Orphée*, the thunderous swiftly-erupting motocyclists slay Cégeste, on the order of Death.

The earliest publication of Cocteau was a volume of verse: *La Lampe d'Aladin*, of 1909, and one of his last publications was poetry: *Paraprosodies*, of 1958. A span of fifty years, during which twenty-one separate books of poems were published, as well as several volumes of selected poems. From the edition of his complete works, Cocteau eliminated the first three volumes of his poetry: *La Lampe d'Aladin*, *Le Prince frivole* (1910), and *La Danse de Sophocle* (1912). The first collection he wished to keep was war poems written between 1916 and 1919, *Le Cap de bonne espérance*, published in 1919, and dedicated to Roland Garros, *prisonnier en Allemagne*. The typography of this long poem suggests the acrobatic flights of the aviator Garros. The symbolism of these flights is the attempt on the part of the poet to escape beyond what is visible, to reach a world above the sensible.

Published in 1920, *Discours du grand sommeil*, is a long poem written between 1916 and 1918. Those critics who had accused Cocteau of an attitude of indifference to the horror of war in his novel *Thomas l'imposteur*, could read in this long poem a work on the suffering of the poet in his meditation on death and friendship and the dismay of mankind at the time of war. The theme of the angel is first introduced, with some development, in *Discours*. The angel is a being who awakens within the poet and speaks to him imperiously. In this early version of the theme, the angel could easily be poetry itself.

A transitional work, *Vocabulaire*, of 1922, is a collection of short poems written prior to the meeting with Radiguet and the experimentation with a new style of greater simplicity and concentration. In *Vocabulaire*, the effort to create a new kind of poetry, an anti-poetry, is too visible. The exercises of these poems were useful in teaching Cocteau ways of reaching a poetic form in which the poem would be severed from the poet, and autonomous in its own purity.

Plain-Chant, of 1923, is the first important poetic work of Cocteau, the reward of a great deal of experimentation, the attainment to a kind of wisdom which is his own, a self-realization when he is able to speak convincingly of his angel and his muses. The form of the poem is more classical, the prosody more regular. The themes of sleep and death are more deeply explored. In *Plain-Chant* they move into full focus as permanent themes in Cocteau's writing.

Concerning the genesis of his important poem, *L'Ange Heurtebise*, of 1925, Cocteau has written in *Journal d'un inconnu* a detailed circumstantial account. The work came about as the ending of a semi-mystical experience, related without much doubt to the death of Radiguet, and was composed in an almost automatic way, by chance, as if the poet were copying down a dictated poem. By comparison with *Plain-Chant*, with which it has affiliations, it is an abstract work, so denuded of a recognizable subject matter that it defies any usual exegesis. The poet speaks of a struggle with a mysterious power within him, which, whenever defeated, returns inexorably to begin again its regime. The poem is words and sounds generated by this force.

Behind many of the poems in Cocteau's next volume, *Opéra*, written between 1925-27, and published in 1927, is the narration of Radiguet's death, the poet's addiction to opium, and the cure he underwent in a sanitarium. The spiritual experience of *L'Ange Heurtebise*, in its absence of images, is not recaptured in *Opéra*, but the two books are closely related. The poems of *Opéra* attempt to express more directly the spectacle that is transpiring within the poet. In a way, these poems are preliminary sketches which will be used in assembling the more complete, the more graphic pictures of *Le Sang d'un poète*. The expression of inner grief gives way to the effects of opium which dissipate it, and this state of euphoria is in turn vanquished by the return of grief and the association of images which bring it back. Even in his use of puns, and in his role of poet-actor, Cocteau is the explorer of himself in *Opéra*, the investigator of his subconscious, the poet who in one line summarizes the harassing paradox of the man who in his social life has to lie *(je suis un mensonge)* and who, as the man, in his discoveries of the poems, speaks the truth *(qui dit toujours la vérité)*.

Je suis un mensonge qui dit toujours la vérité. The falseness of appearance is always contradicted by the inner truth.

After several years during which Cocteau's activities were centered on the theatre, he returned to the writing of poetry, to the composing of *Léone*, of 1945. In this long poem, in which the world of sleep predominates, the female figure of Léone moves about in close relationship with the poet. She is a character resembling characters created by Cocteau in other works, and at the same time a new character playing the poet's most intimate drama. At the end of the poem, Léone is called the muse, but the mystery of her identity is preserved.

Written at almost the same time as *Léone, La Crucifixion* (1946) is the harshest, the most dissonant, and the most difficult of Cocteau's poems. To the suffering of the soul is added the suffering of the flesh. All lyrical quality has been suppressed, and only a cry is audible from the beginning to the end. The poet with his pain is alone.

Ten years later, in *Clair-obscur* (1956), Cocteau published a long collection of characteristic poems. Themes and forms long associated with him are here developed. The critics pointed out the facility of the poems, without remembering that Cocteau's art has always seemed facile, that it is often a mask for the writer's labor. They also judged harshly the repetition of certain themes without remembering that each book of Cocteau is a reaffirmation of such themes as sleep and death where friendship takes refuge.

In describing his book of 1957: *Paraprosodies précédées de sept dialogues*, Cocteau used the term "automatic," as he had earlier with *L'Ange Heurtebise*. But this designates the strict mathematics of syllabification and rhythm, of rhyme and alliteration, rather than the "automatic writing" of surrealism. This exterior rigor is that of a machine, which will allow the spirit its full freedom. It is an exercise in asceticism which will permit the poet to explore the night out of which the poem comes, a problem which preoccupied Cocteau during a large part of his career. This "'night" would seem to be, for the poet, much more than the subconscious, as defined by Freud. Poetic form is a door opening out on to a landscape. But the reader has to push open the door. The landscape is always the unknown, even to the poet.

Soon after the turn of the century, at a time when Jean Cocteau was still a child, the art of poetry in France underwent an important change. With the poems of Apollinaire, Blaise Cendrars, and Max Jacob, the art rejected its classical canons of logic and strict prosody. Inspired especially by the examples of Rimbaud and Laforgue, the new poets, whom Cocteau was to know and emulate, initiated a double quest: a search, carried on simultaneously, for their own identification. This search led them into the new domains of adventure, of the subconscious, and of madness. Cocteau's position as a poet is closely related to the achievements of Apollinaire and Jacob, and later with the work of such a poet as Robert Desnos. Cocteau also opened up new territories of experience, new experimentations in which the search for poetry and the exploration of the poet's subconscious coincided.

The break with the parnassian ideal, with the rigor of traditional prosody, was consummated about 1912, at the time when *Alcools* of Apollinaire was about to be published, and when Blaise Cendrars returned from his trip to New

York, with his poem *Pâques à New York*. These works testify to the noisy upheavals of poetry in the years just preceding the First World War. And Cocteau published his first poetry at exactly this time. He too helped to break down the barrages which had held poetry in. The new poetry resembled an overflow, an escape in all directions to new lands.

Poetry within itself constructs another mystery remaining beside the human mystery it tries to comprehend. It does not attempt to *explain* the human mystery as prose does, because it is not discursive in its highest form. It finds its form by a series of short-cuts and detours, and leads finally to a landscape that is new and isolated. The poems of Cocteau have no relationship with other landscapes, with the work of other poets. They are recognizable as being Cocteau's. In writing them he consulted only himself, he encountered only himself. Their verbal mechanism is his own invention. This process is the way by which one poet is totally distinguishable from all others. Any stanza from *Mémoire* of Rimbaud could not possibly be confused with any other poet. Any four lines from *L'Après-midi d'un faune* could not be ascribed to any poet except Mallarmé. In the same way, the swiftness of tempo, the bareness, the serious wit, the arch simplicity of Cocteau's writing are signatures in his most successful poems which no one else could claim. The poem is, finally, the means by which the poet transcends the common mediocrity of life. It is the reduction and the justification of what is daily and destined to disappear. It abolishes the law of mortality, of everything destined to disappear, in its discovery of the laws of poetry. The muse exerted a very real tyranny over Cocteau. She is no invisible symbolic figure for him. She is the protagonist.

A city poet, as opposed to a nature poet, Cocteau is even more a poet of apartment and rooms, of those places where solitude encourages ghosts and abstract monologues with a

night world. The stage and the poem are both for Cocteau
the site of demonstrations calculated to startle spectator and
reader. Familiar objects utilized by him take on surprising
proportions and meanings. The poems are presentations,
miniature scenes where enigmas and strange conjunctions
work miracles in words. Everything is used and applied:
friendship, opium, a conversion; each theme is expounded
until it becomes a reality. Cocteau finds for whatever transpires within his mind a story and the story converts the
mental picture or the abstract idea into a poem. It is always
close to the miraculous, to the surreal. The critic Jean Cassou
once called Cocteau "our Nostradamus," in his apparent role
of astrologer and alchemist.

The effects produced by some of the paintings of Giorgio
di Chirico are not unlike those produced by the most successful poems of Cocteau. When Chirico assembles on the same
canvas a Greek temple and a mirror wardrobe, he forces us
into some alienation of habit. The supernatural story of the
Annunciation is changed into a simple village tale when
Cocteau relates it in just twelve lines, and the Virgin is the
lass who hides her face in shame and shock at the news of
the angel.

GABRIEL AU VILLAGE

Mademoiselle Marie
Vous êtes grosse, dit l'ange,
Vous aurez un fils sans mari
Pardonnez si je vous dérange

Cette façon d'annoncer
Les choses par la fenêtre,
Etonne un peu la fiancée
Qui son amour voudrait connaître.

L'ange s'en va, comme fonte
Des neiges, vers l'inhumain.
La petite a un peu honte
Et se cache dans ses mains.

Many traditions of French art are in this typical poem of Cocteau: the swift elegance and lightness of tone of Voltaire, its ellipsis and delicate poignancy which could be found fifty years earlier in the *poèmes de circonstance* of Mallarmé. It is as detached from the poet, as a drawing is detached from Picasso. It is fragile in its minimum of subject matter, but it is able to stand by itself. Behind the real scene in *Gabriel au village*, depicted with familiarity, one can barely make out a sketch of the unknown, of the supernatural. The analogy is not forced, but it is there. Life and death are both present in the brief poems as well as in the major works.

However disguised it may be, the pathos in the poems diminishes their effect of "precious" poems. It is often pathos made acceptable by wit, whereby a very tenuous relationship is established between ideas that usually have little in common one with the other. The common theme, at times visible and at other times invisible, in the poems of Cocteau, is the human mystery. But the poems are units by themselves, each one of which has its own logic. Each is a shortened translation of a continuous melody, of a continuous thought. What the poet proves over and over again is not the profundity of the human mystery but the deftness of the artisan who knows how to reduce and justify his inner life. Whatever signal he receives from the cosmos and from the cosmos of his heart, he transmits with words and rhythms that never inflate nor betray the original message.

In *Le Cap de bonne espérance*, the constant use of the airplane testifies not only to the pilot's escape from the world, but to the role of poetry by means of which the poet moves very far away and high up. It is a bodily release. The physical sensation of rhythm and rhyme is a way of breaking off from the familiar ties with the world. The art of aviation is a facile symbol for the twentieth-century dandy, for the young man who has to separate himself swiftly and totally from the world of accepted values and stifling agreements and commitments, in order to project himself into the rarefied atmosphere of superiority and of solitude. The movement of the dandy is always upward and away. His goal is that inner perfection, that estrangement from the commonplace, of which clothes and speech and manners are merely symbols. Cocteau's first self-justification was his flight in the airplane of Roland Garros to that sphere where, stripped of all the accoutrements that had grown useless, he could start afresh on what was to be the second phase of his life.

Le Discours du grand sommeil is the fall back to earth, to the murkiest, muddiest, most terrestrial part of the earth: the trenches of World War I. It was a plunge downward, and a contact with the grim presence of physical death. After the soaring speed of the airplane, came the immobilization of death, the inert sleep of Icarus! The poem is described by Cocteau as "translated from that dead language, of that dead country, where my friends are dead." The poet gives over to the currents in which he is caught, to the inevitable.

The angel speaks in Discours du grand sommeil and demands that the poet who carries him appear as if he had no knowledge of this. Sleep is heroic because it occurs in the midst of a war. Everything is antithesis, everything is a force struggling against another force: the past and the present; the prince who is a soldier; the demolisher who wants to rebuild. Words and their opposites are more vigilantly controlled by Cocteau at this time in French poetry, when Dada was turning into surrealism and poets were joining words that had no relationship one with the other.

In the volume Poésies of 1920, the poems are less bare, less elliptical. If the poetic form is more traditional, there is little trace of poetic influence. Cocteau's poems are the result of his direct contacts with life, of his own experiences.

Ode à Pablo Picasso is a course on the new aesthetics, in the form of a poem. The new artist performs in full view of the public. He has nothing up his sleeves, nothing in his pockets:

> Rien dans les manches   Rien dans les poches

Cocteau ends the poem swiftly by asking for a hat from the audience to be used by the Harlequin of Port-Royal.

> Un monsieur
> voudrait-il prêter son chapeau
> à l'arlequin de Port-Royal.

In his essay on Picasso (*Le Rappel à l'ordre*), Cocteau designates the painter as the Harlequin of Port-Royal, and thus joins the pantomime theme in the paintings with the Jansenist severity of the painter's style.

Throughout *Poésies* Cocteau experiments with his art and trains himself. His temperament, volatile and frenzied, is matched by his intelligence, which comprehends every aspect of his human drama. The combination of this temperament and this intelligence is the poetic work which grows more supple and more substantial as the volumes follow one another. Cyclists, dancers, angels are athletic names for the poet. They are his trainers who keep him in form, who teach him how to develop his muscles and who teach him also ways to avoid showing his muscular strength.

The final poem of the book is *Mouchoir*, the sign of farewell, and is literally that: a farewell to those who had been with him on that part of the voyage: He sends them back to the ship, where poetry is, as he faces alone something new, something unknown. He greets a new city:

> Bonjour, mon métropolitain!

and drowns out a nostalgia for earlier cities:

> J'étouffe un vieux regret de mes villes d'avant.

Art is constant renovation. The artist has to operate on himself and remove all useless organs. He has to move ahead into the future work, even if he has no ship, no vehicle with which he can easily reach the next goal:

> Mais puis-je partir sans rames, sans essence . . .

With *Vocabulaire*, Cocteau's private mythology is fully established, the words with which he had defined his vocation, and by means of which he carries on a severe commerce with the muses. Comparisons and symbols are methods by which to express the most intimate sentiments of the poet, and which are eternal sentiments. Birds and angels are the figures moving through these verses, delegated to justify the poet's adventure. At times they accompany him and at times they merge with him in a fantasy-identification. The image of snow turning into marble, or ink turning into poems, or bees secreting honey in their hives is the persistent theme of metamorphosis: the central function of the poet. "Central" because it is the process by which life turns into death, and the process by which death, in its permanent form, redeems life. The entire work of Cocteau is permeated with this experience. In order to translate it, in order to make it felt by his readers, he devises image after image to testify to this change that obsesses his mind. He would seem to be saying, first to himself, because he is the one obsessed, and then to everyone else who will listen, that if this process can be accepted, the enigma of existence itself, of love and aspiration, of victory and defeat, will be solved.

The metamorphosis is always startling and gigantic: as

from a live swan twisting its neck and changing into a statue of salt:

> Tords-toi le cou noble statue
> De sel, halte! retourne-toi

Each stanza of this poem, *Mort d'un cygne*, contains a juxta-position of opposites, a movement of gigantic change which is either illusion or disillusion. A white cloud, for example, is called Gilles (the famous clown of the eighteenth century painted by Watteau) opening his satin arms. But the poet wonders if it might be Gilles de Rais (the murderer who will redden the morning sky):

> Nuage blanc êtes-vous Gilles,
> Ecartant ses bras de satin,
> Ou Gilles de Rais, plus habile
> A rougir le ciel du matin?

The poem *A force de plaisirs* is characteristic of the most successful in *Vocabulaire*, where the key words are quite specifically the obsessions of Cocteau: bees, as the time-consuming activities of the poet's life, and their empty hive resembling a house of crime:

> Que fites-vous de mal, abeilles de ma vie?
> Votre ruche déserte étant maison de crime

For predestined hands, snow can quickly turn into marble. Such an image is Cocteau's signature in such works as *Le Sang d'un poète* and *Les Enfants terribles*, and in the poem it announces a road taken in reverse direction: the marble statue turns to salt and the salt turns to living flesh on the beach where Sunday bathers are visible:

> La neige est vite marbre aux mains prédestinées;
> Du marbre au Sel Vénus connaît la route blanche,
> Et du sel à la chair enfin la voilà née
> Sur la plage où chacun se baigne le Dimanche.

Plain-Chant, of 1923, is a long poem on the combined themes of sleep, love, and death, one of the most serious poems that Cocteau ever wrote, one of the most unified in tone and texture. It is the long aria-like poem, as central in the work of Cocteau as *Le Voyage* in Baudelaire, *Le Bateau ivre* in Rimbaud, *La Chanson du mal-aimé* in Apollinaire. The surface of the poem, its outer form, is extraordinarily smooth, for the tumultuous, deeply felt experiences it covers. The classical qualities of the form have permitted the poet to give himself over to the powers that have tormented him, and he does more in *Plain-Chant* in the way of personal confession than in any other single piece of writing. The powers of the dark, of sleep and of watching the sleeper, allow him to inhabit simultaneously the world of the living and the world of the dead.

Sleep is the embalmer and the dream of the sleeper is an Egypt: the poet lives the terror of such false serenity:

> Rien ne m'effraye plus que la fausse accalmie
> D'un visage qui dort;
> Ton rêve est une Egypte et toi c'est la momie
> Avec ton masque d'or.

The poet and his other self *(mon ange)* are close to the sea. It is the setting of *Plain-Chant:* an element as vast as the element of sleep. The drama of sleep and death is the same, because the poet cannot follow the beloved within that element.

> Le sommeil et la mer sont tes vrais éléments . . .
> Hélas! tu le sais trop, je ne peux pas t'y suivre . . .

The distress in Cocteau's life over the death of Raymond Radiguet induced him to seek escape in the experience of opium. The period spent in Villefranche marks a turning point in his work as a poet, which is the subject of *Opéra* and of the poem *L'Ange Heurtebise*, published in 1925 with a photograph of Man Ray. It is a difficult text because the poet is describing transcendental experiences by means of very concrete objects, by a vocabulary that deflates any attempt at lyricism. The rhythm is broken as all illusions are broken.

The poet calls upon Angel Heurtebise to come down again to help him in his solitude. Each month this angel is killed, shot down by the angels of God.

> Ange ou feu? Trop tard. En joue
> Feu!
> Il tombe fusillé par les soldats de Dieu

In stanza twelve the familiar words are recited, are conjugated: death, angel, Heurtebise, the ace card, the pack of cards, the swan, and the new name is announced, the new angel Cégeste, who is to replace Heurtebise:

> La mort de l'ange Heurtebise
> Fut la mort de l'ange, la mort
> Heurtebise fut une mort d'ange,
> Une mort d'ange Heurtebise,
> Un mystère du change, un as
> Qui manque au jeu, un crime
> Que le pampre enlace, un cep
> De lune, un chant de cygne qui mord,
> Un autre ange le remplace dont je
> Ne savais pas le nom hier;
> En dernière heure: Cégeste.

The earlier definition of "angelism" which appears in *Secret professionnel*, finds its application in *L'Ange Heurtebise*. The poet has to reach an angelic disinterestedness which some may call egoism. Whatever attracts him violently in the way of earthly pleasure will be scorned and left behind. The angel-poet, ange Heurtebise, is beyond morality, detached

from the suffering and the consequences of morality when he
is a poet. Arthur Rimbaud remained steadfastly, for Cocteau,
the example of angel on earth because of his capacity to
embrace the violence of pleasure and to leave it with the
swiftness of a winged creature who actually inhabits a realm
above the earth.

Opéra, the volume of 1927, to which was added *L'Ange
Heurtebise*, opens with poems as serene as those in *Plain-
Chant*, and continues with pieces where allusions to angelism
and opium predominate. The major poems in the collection,
such as *Prière mutilée*, are struggles between the poet and his
angel to reach some state of peace in self-knowledge. He is
living close to "the system of heaven," almost within its confines, so close that he can feel divine presences moving about
actively. Angels appear from their embassy. As they climb
hills, they raise their robes. The mirrors into which the poet
looks are suddenly too small because they are filled with the
elegance of the angels. This fourth stanza testifies to the action of the entire poem. Supernatural forces are amassed to
invade the poet:

> Les anges relevant leurs jupes ralenties
> Escaladaient les collines, les palissades;
> Et l'incroyable élégance de cette ambassade
> Remplissait les miroirs devenus trop petits.

Each of the poems disperses all the others. Cocteau never
stops for long. The struggle with the angel and the opium
dream (cf. *Prairie légère*) are momentary halts. Poetry has
to be progress and conquest.

Jean Cocteau belongs to that tradition of French poets
who renew themselves from book to book, who move, not
from style to style, but to varieties of their style which corre-
spond to moments in their lives, to experiences which move
and form them. It is the tradition of Ronsard and Hugo; it is

especially the tradition of Verlaine. Each volume of these poets is a halt, a form perfected in accord with one moment in their life story. The other tradition, which today enjoys greater favor, is the tradition of the one book, of the poet who at the beginning of his career, found himself so totally expressed that his art stopped there: Villon, of the two *Testaments*, Baudelaire of *Les Fleurs du Mal*, Rimbaud and Mallarmé, poets of one book each, and Saint-John Perse in the twentieth century. There are resemblances between *Plain-Chant* and *Léone*, between *L'Ange Heurtebise* and *La Crucifixion*, but each book is a distinct halt, a distinct moment wherein some profound experience was threatened by sleep or death. It is a long cataclysmic work of images and propositions, of themes that are almost always conceived of as being threats.

La Crucifixion (1946) is one of the most plastic poems of Cocteau, where physical pain is depicted in drawn figures. The twenty-five stanzas are abrupt and bare and irregular. Nouns often exist without verbs in order to accentuate their pain and the traps of pain. In the eighth stanza, the crucifixion is seen as an infernal machine of exact calculation. The stage hands are in the wings with their ladders. For all eternity this machine has been controlling in outer space the candelabrum of the stars.

> La machine infernale était mue
> par des calculs
> ignorés des machinistes
> d'une coulisse d'échelles
> interdites aux ramoneurs
> sous peine de mort. De toute
> éternité mue au coeur
> même du drame la machine
> d'une précision écoeurante
> réglait en outre
> le candélabre des astres

Léone (1942-44), a poem published one year before *La Crucifixion*, transpires within the world of sleep and within the confines of dreams. Without leaving his bed, the poet follows Léone, a supernatural creature closely resembling Death in *Orphée*. She leads him through Paris, a sleeping city, and through unnamed places where legendary lovers—Tristan and Isolde, for example—are consumed with love for all time. She comes to spaces where stars are in combat with one another. The poet cannot disobey this muse-like figure of Léone. She is a female Heurtebise as she leads the poet beside characters he had once created, and as she gradually grows into the leading character of the poet's personal drama.

In stanza thirty-three the same question asked in *Orphée* is repeated: Who is Léone and whose orders is she obeying? When the poet awakens, does Léone walk in some other sleep?

> Peut-être qu'enjambant le choc de mon réveil
> Léone marchera dans un autre sommeil.
> De sommeil en sommeil elle ira sans démordre
> Jusqu'à celui dont elle exécute les ordres.
> Quel est-il?

Typical of the variety of places visited by the poet is stanza seventy-five, where he sees the moonlight on the parapets of Elsinore and where his ghost is Hamlet, and Léone is the king:

> Elseneur! Lieu de lune et de chemins de ronde
> On y voyait le roi pénétrer l'autre monde,
> Mon ombre était Hamlet et Léone le roi.

Published in 1952, *Le Chiffre Sept* is a long poem, less narrative and less descriptive than *Léone*, in which Cocteau reveals a dual form of suffering. First, that suffering of the artist imposed by the Muses who are cruel and demanding.

In some of his earliest prose writing, Cocteau had referred to the Muses in this way, but with more wit and lightness than in *Le Chiffre Sept*. And second, the suffering imposed upon him by a world of selfishness and blindness, by a world that seems determined to destroy him. This theme had been briefly projected in *Orphée*, in both the play and the film, but in the new poem, the world is seen as absurdly centered on self-destruction. There is more bitterness, more pessimism in *Le Chiffre Sept* than in other poetic works of Cocteau. The lyric quality is more vibrant, more full. Waiting rooms and law courts are spoken of as being decorated with geraniums whose red is the poet's blood:

> Salle des pas perdus, portes de la justice,
> Chambres où l'accusé se change en innocent,
> Embellissez vos cours (vous me rendrez service)
> De ces géraniums qui décorent mon sang.

The poem was written at the instigation of the publisher-poet Pierre Seghers, and it is in many ways Cocteau's meditation on his life. The theme of chance, announced in the title, is the invisible, intangible poem that directs the poet's existence, that is disguised in the words of the writer, in all the familiar objects the poet has appropriated through the years, such as those mirrors that do not want to be passed through.

> *Miroirs qui détestez qu'on vous passe au travers.*

The stringent quality and the bitterness of *Le Chiffre Sept* are absent from the collection *Clair-obscur*. The ninety-two stanzas of this poem record an attitude of balance and serenity where the poet moves easily between the two worlds of light and shadow. An epigraph of Jean-Philippe Rameau admirably summarizes the aesthetics of Jean Cocteau, of which *Clair-obscur* is a good example: *Il est difficile d'avoir*

l'air facile. The facile appearance of gracefulness, in a poem
of Cocteau, or in a drawing of Matisse, camouflages the
difficulty of labor that preceded the work. The final economy
of the work is the result of great lavishness of effort. The
swiftness and wit of final effects come after prolonged
intensity.

To the critic André Fraigneau, who wrote the very sympa-
thetic study, *Cocteau par lui-même* (1957), the poet confided
that *Clair-obscur* was written between two periods of serious
illness which undoubtedly had some effect on the work. To a
large degree, however, suffering and discouragement have
been suppressed in the poem. Cocteau's mastery of the means
is in itself a sublimation. Jean Cocteau is as fully in *Clair-
obscur*, of 1954, as he is in *Plain-Chant* of 1922. After an
interval of thirty years, the same spirit of youthfulness permitted him to create that kind of art whose appearance is
facility.

In the second part of *Clair-obscur*, Cocteau pays homage
to several Spanish artists: Greco, Velasquez, Goya, the poet
Gongora, the toreador Manolete. And then his homage is
paid to many different writers: Kafka, Pushkin, Jarry,
Rilke, Mallarmé. The poems are brief but they indicate
something of the complexity of the subjects. Each poem is a
portrait or an attempt to describe the inspiration of the artist.

Cocteau's preoccupation with the meaning of poetry, with
the reasons for writing poetry, was constant throughout his
life and he often expressed his thoughts on such problems in
aesthetics when invited to speak publicly, as in Oxford in
1956 on receiving an honorary doctor's degree. Poetry is a
labyrinth and the poet is held by two conflicting sentiments:
by a fear of confronting the monster in the labyrinth and by
a devouring curiosity to see him. Cocteau has also called

poetry a terrifying solitude, a curse that comes at birth, a spiritual sickness. It is, especially, the reverse of what most people consider poetic: it is a secret weapon. Whatever thought a poem contains, it is derived from the words themselves. It is not the mere embellishment of ideas.

In order to illustrate poetry's particular power of communication, Cocteau referred to a custom among simple peasants in the Antillas. If a woman in the country wanted to communicate with her husband or son in the town, she would say her message to a tree, and the husband or son would bring to her whatever she requested. When one of the women was asked why she used a tree, she replied: "Because I am poor. If I were rich, I would have a telephone."

The secret language, characteristic of each poet, accounts for the solitude that surrounds a poem. It accounts for the scandal and the exhibitionism that appear so often traits of poetry. The sentence that Cocteau wrote for *Le Potomak* in 1915 states an important part of his aesthetics: "You should cultivate whatever the public reproaches you for, because it is you." (*Ce que le public te reproche, cultive-le, c'est toi.*) In such a sentence, Cocteau implies that poets are often honored by their failures, and dishonored by their successes. Bad luck (Baudelaire called it *le guignon*) may turn out to be a consecration, and good luck may be the devil in disguise bent upon ruining the poet under the pretext of paying him homage.

Each poem, each book of poems of Cocteau, is a fresh start. It is also a continuity in creative work. He is the opposite of the traditional lyric poet who sings of ecstasy, of the imprecision of feelings, of the occult in its manifestations. Poetry is exactness, because it answers a need. The line is brief, bare, limpid. Labor is involved in bringing about the passage from a man's secrets to the light of the work. The poet is archeologist far more than he is a prestidigitator. And the poet's vocation is one of strict morality, of solitude, of humility, of obstinate self-discipline. No matter what is the final tone of a poem, each poem is serious and the poet writing it is engaged in a risk at each moment. He is bringing to light a reality which is adjacent to the habitually real.

The poet's ego, who is finally responsible for the poem, is a mysterious being concealed from the world because he lives in a kind of darkness and is not very well known by the other self of the poet, the familiar self. Cocteau always looked upon the poet's ego as operating alone, in a separate world, as distant from daily occupations as the world of sleep is distant from the world of a man's consciousness. Cocteau has explained that at the end of a serious illness, he wrote the poem *Le Requiem*, under the direction of the inner self. Willfully and unwillfully he always refrained from writing the brilliant kind of verse, the easily flowing verse. He called *Le Requiem* a river of blood that changed to ink and that now flows into that mysterious sea called the public.

In one of the final interviews, in 1962, Cocteau recapitulated a sentence he had often expressed: there is no greater solitude than a poem *(il n'y a pas de plus grande solitude qu'un poème)* and added, "especially a poem written in French." When asked to explain this thought, he said that France is a great creative country, but not an attentive country. Frenchmen are like those florists who hate flowers. More than any other type of writer, the poet is disliked. Cocteau refers to masterpieces that remained invisible as long as their creators lived.

On the publication of *Le Requiem*, one of the most familiar attacks was again levelled against Cocteau, that of writing in every genre possible, that of dispersing himself and diluting his talent. Cocteau's persistent answer to this charge has been the power of poetry to take all forms, to borrow all vehicles. He does not separate his poems from his films and plays, from his essays and novels and drawings. The paintings in the chapel of Villefranche are part of his poetry, as well as the seven stained-glass windows in Metz, and the sets and costumes for *Pelléas et Mélisande*. When he worked with his hands, he rested from writing; and when he wrote, he rested from painting.

Poetry was indispensable for Cocteau, but he never said indispensable for what. It is an art with words, as old as mankind, and yet the object created by the words remains invisible. Cocteau has called it by all possible names: a royal ghost walking about in his life and a secret illness. He was a poet, but no more concerned with poetry than a plant is concerned with horticulture. Nature and its prodigality with seeds is comparable to the poet and his prodigality of verses written and unwritten. But the earth economizes and nurtures only one seed out of countless seeds, so that the species will be preserved. When one poem is successful and separated from all others, it is bare and unknown, and will be visited by shepherds and magi.

VIII
THE POET
AS FILM MAKER

W HEN, IN 1930, Cocteau was working on *Le Sang d'un poète*, he had no intention of making it into a commercial enterprise. Later, in the forties, with such a film as *L'éternel retour*, he did look upon film making as a means of reaching a wide public. But in 1930, the film he originally called *La vie d'un poète*, was a means of expression, a means of experimentation, an almost personal way of self-expression. The film was subsidized by le vicomte Charles de Noailles, who gave Cocteau one million francs. (He had also given a million francs to Luis Bunuel for *L'Age d'Or*.) The gift entailed no commitments. Cocteau was totally free, responsible only to himself.

The story of *Le Sang d'un poète* is the inner life of a poet, taking place during the time that elapses between the beginning of the fall of a factory chimney and the collapse of the chimney. As soon as we see the chimney begin to totter, we hear Cocteau's voice say: *Tandis que tonnaient au loin les canons de Fontenoy, dans une modeste chambre, un jeune homme. . . .* While the world is engaged in violent events, the poet is attentive solely to what is transpiring within himself.

The poet is always for Cocteau any kind of creator, and in this case he is a painter, a man (resembling Rudolph Valentino) drawing a portrait. This first episode is called *La main blessée ou la cicatrice du poète*. The portrait comes to life and opens its mouth. When the poet tries to blot out the mouth, it is impressed on his hand. A friend calling is disgusted with what he sees and leaves abruptly. The poet remains alone with his own creation. The next morning he finds in his room a life-sized statue of a woman. He applies the wound on his hand to the statue's face, and the statue comes to life. She forbids him to go out, and removes all windows and door. She asks the poet if it is not absurd to awaken a statue from its sleep of centuries.

At the beginning of the second episode, called *Les murs ont-ils des oreilles?*, the statue asks him if he thinks it is easy to get rid of a wound and suggests that he walk through the mirror. *Crois-tu qu'il est si simple de se débarrasser d'une blessure? Il te reste une ressource. Entrer dans la glace et t'y promener.* When the poet answers that people do not walk through mirrors (*on n'entre pas dans les glaces*), she replies: "You wrote that people go through mirrors and you do not believe it." (*Tu as écrit qu'on entrait dans les glaces et tu n'y croyais pas.*) This is a reference to Cocteau's play of 1926, *Orphée*. So, the poet does dive into the mirror, where he finds the myths of his subconscious, episodes examined through the eye of a keyhole: the death of a Mexican, a flying lesson, an opium-smoker, an hermaphrodite. When the poet returns to his room, he smashes the statue into bits, as a voice says: "In breaking statues, you risk becoming one yourself." *A casser des statues, on risque d'en devenir une soi-même.*

In the third episode we see the poet's statue in the cité

Monthiers, a small street in the ninth *arrondissement* of Paris, between the rue d'Amsterdam and the rue de Clichy. A group of school children destroy the statue with snow balls as easily as if it were made of snow. The boys quarrel among themselves until one is fatally wounded in the chest. At this point Cocteau's voice recites a poem, *Le Camarade*, which appears today in his volume of verse *Opéra*. It is about the blows dealt in school fights, blows as hard as snowballs which cause blood to flow. This episode, *La bataille des boules de neige*, is a memory of Cocteau's lycée Condorcet.

The fourth and last episode: *la carte volée*, is the same setting of the cité Monthiers. The balcony windows have turned into theatre boxes that are filled with people. Beside the child's body stands a table where the poet is playing cards with a lady who resembles the statue. She fans herself as if detached or indifferent, and the poet, in order to win, cheats. He puts his hand under the boy's jacket and pulls out the ace of hearts. But the boy's guardian angel performs another trick, recovers the ace of hearts and disappears with the body. The woman then says: "If you do not have the ace of hearts, you have lost out." (*Si vous n'avez pas l'as de coeur, mon cher, vous êtes un homme perdu.*) This may be an allusion to Raymond Radiguet's death, whom Cocteau, in his poem *L'Ange Heurtebise*, calls the ace which the pack of cards did not have.

When the poet takes his life, and we can see the blood on his cheeks and lips, there is applause from the boxes. The ending of the film is an allegory on immortality: the bull, the map of Europe (Europa) on the bull, the poet's lyre floating through space. *La route est longue*, we hear. The long road is the mortal boredom of immortality: *l'ennui mortel de l'immortalité*.

In many ways, *Le Sang d'un poète* is close in ideas, in its analysis of the poet's myth, to the earlier play *Orphée*. Thanks to film technique, Cocteau presents the work as if it were the unfolding of a dream. It is a descent into the self and there the creative secrets are revealed. A poet has to pass through a series of deaths before reaching his definitive death, which is immortality. But everything is proposed to us as if it were an enigma that we can see only through mirrors or keyholes.

The chimney that starts to topple at the beginning of the film, and that falls at the end, is an effort to transcribe the mystery of time. Cocteau seems to be saying that time is an illusion for man that exists between his birth and death. Both the play *Orphée*, which preceded it by a few years, and the film *Le Sang d'un poète*, demonstrate Cocteau's liking for enigma, his tendency to demonstrate truth under the mask of a fable, and his manner of mingling the dream world with the real world.

When, in 1930, Cocteau undertook the creation of *Le Sang d'un poète*, he had already rejuvenated several artistic forms, and stamped them with his own temperament and vision: the novel, plays, essays, the ballet, graphic arts. The only one left was the movies. He was determined not to create any facile diversion for the typical movie public, but to use the film as a means of expressing his own thought. He used it as a poet and designer experimenting with a new art.

Le Sang is a commentary on the very private mythology of Jean Cocteau, on themes that today seem less private because they have appeared in other works of Cocteau: *Orphée*, *Opéra*, *Les Enfants terribles*. The charge of unintelligibility is no longer made. In watching the film, it is imperative not to forget Cocteau's preface, where he says that poetry is a coat of arms whose symbols can be deciphered only after a loss of blood. He dedicates his film to those painters of escutcheons and coats of arms: to Paolo Uccello, to Piera della Francesco, and to Pisanello.

Le Belle et la bête, of 1945, is another film written and directed by Cocteau. Although it is based on the fairy story of Jeanne-Marie Le Prince de Beaumont, the film is a new work, a tragedy formulated by Cocteau against a seventeenth-century background. The character Belle, reminiscent of Snow White and Cinderella, incarnates kindness toward her father and toward la Bête. The young girl and the monster each lives in her or his own world. The tragedy is the separation of the two, the incapacity of the lover joining with the one he loves. Belle's love for la Bête deepens through the story and gives it its dimension of tragedy. As soon as Belle is separated from the monster, everything changes. Her friendship, her kindness become passionate. The sumptuousness of the production is largely due to Christian Bérard, who was responsible for the setting and the costumes. The scenes in the father's home might easily be an evocation of Vermeer, and those in the monster's palace are reminiscent of the mysterious lavishness of a Doré painting.

In 1948, Cocteau produced two films closely based on two of his plays: L'Aigle à deux têtes and Les Parents terribles. The first was far less successful than the second. The text of L'Aigle was drastically reduced, and the film turned into a melodrama, a kind of mystery play in costume. But Les Parents terribles remains more faithful to the text and the performances of the play. The tragedy of the family, of the apartment closed off from the world, is dramatized by a skillful use of the camera. The emotional conflicts revealed on the faces of the characters, the close study of their gestures and the objects surrounding them are caught by the camera. The hardness of Léo and the madness of the mother Yvonne are as poignantly shown as the youthfulness of Michel. The camera explores the secrets of the drama more profoundly than the stage performance was able to do.

Whereas *Le Sang d'un poète* was a work created directly as a film in 1930, *Les Enfants terribles* was a film of 1950, adapted from Cocteau's novel of 1929. Technically the films are very different, but thematically they have resemblances.

Every possible theory has been proposed to explain this enigmatic novel, a story which opens with the snowball which the pupil Dargelos throws at his classmate Paul, on leaving school one day, and ends with the dark ball of poison which Dargelos years later sends to Paul.

The book was a consciously conceived, consciously written story. There are many realistic details in it from Cocteau's childhood: memories of the cité Monthiers, the little street used in *Le Sang d'un poète*, the characters of the brother and sister, the setting of their room. These are all striking elements, and they come from real life. And then there is the more abstract theme of destiny, of tragic destiny, that becomes apparent especially at the end.

The book, from the moment of its first appearance, until today, has had an exceptional success. It is probably the best known, the best liked single work of Cocteau. The loftiness of its tone, of its style may be the explanation for this success. Each successive generation of young readers discovers the book and finds in it, not a mirror of a generation, but a picture capable of suggesting the drama and the destiny of young people. The brother and sister, Paul and Elisabeth, have a purity about them, in their will to remain faithful to their destiny, even if this destiny leads them into a tragic end. Their integrity would seem to be their childhood which they

Les Enfants terribles, with Edouard Dermit in the role of Paul

insist upon preserving. The tragic role of the novel is Elisabeth, the child-sister.

The young readers appropriated the book for themselves,
though Cocteau always disclaimed any feeling of solidarity
with his younger readers, and always denied the existence of
any message in the novel. What attracts the book's readers
even today is the commentary it makes on human fate or
destiny that cannot be tricked or altered by time, by human
time that brings with it growth and forgetfulness. Nothing is
forgotten between the opening episode of the snowball and
the closing episode of the black ball of poison. This theme of
the white and black ball at the beginning and the end of
Les Enfants terribles is comparable to the falling chimney
that announces and concludes *Le Sang d'un poète*. Dargelos
the class bully, who throws the white snowball at the beginning of *Les Enfants terribles* is the same who, years later,
poisons his same victim by sending him the black pellet.
Destiny is victorious over the lies which the distance of time
and space tells us.

When, in 1950, Cocteau adapted his novel into a film by
writing the scenario, the dialogue, and the commentaries, he
was helped in the actual shooting of the film by Jean-Pierre
Melville. The film of *Les Enfants terribles*, despite its beauty,
is inferior to the novel. The poetic, tragic strangeness of the
novel appears in the film as something eccentric or melo-
dramatic. In his way of telling the story, the novelist sustains
the mysteriousness of tragic destiny, whereas the art of the
cinematographer is not always able to avoid the merely picturesque. From time to time in the film, Cocteau's own voice
speaks sentences destined to unite and explain sequences, but
even this technique is not always able to recapture the quality
of legend, of the irremediable, which the novel sustains from
beginning to end. And yet the beauty of this film is undeni-

able. Nicole Stéphane plays the part of Elisabeth, and in the very intense scene of her crime, when she climbs and descends the stairway, there is a beauty of movement and dignity and suspense, but in the passage in the book, Cocteau has succeeded in changing the real world and making it into something supernatural. The camera remains too close to the anecdote, but the novel avoids all the triviality of the story in order to create the spell of the epic.

The final scene of the film is unquestionably an attempt on the part of Cocteau and Melville to remain as close as possible to the final scene of the novel. The anguish of Elisabeth, which precedes the dénouement, is composed of many elements in the novel which are difficult for an actress to portray: there is certainly a tinge of madness in her, there is some degree of shame which is constantly vying with pride, and there is finally a sense of power, a will of her energies that force her to take her brother with her into death, and thus free the room where they had lived and where their life was symbolized by a series of talismans. Elisabeth defies everyone and everything in this final gesture. The pictures on the screen do not seem to elevate her as high as the words on the page.

It is perhaps the character of Elisabeth that makes the film almost impossible to create. She is so many characters simultaneously: a child and a demon, a sister and a goddess. In every scene she is being transformed into a power greater than herself, but in the final scene especially, where she succeeds in reigning in an absolute way. The brother and sister at the end inhabit another realm completely separate from the purely human.

The film of *Orphée* of 1950 is a synthesis of the various forms of creative work done by Cocteau between 1930 and

1950. For the second time in his film career—the first was *Le Sang d'un poète*—he made no attempt, no compromise, in order to reach the large movie public. And yet this work, more fervently than any other, has appealed to cinema addicts throughout the world. It is the masterpiece of the poet-cinematographer.

The myth of Orpheus, for Cocteau, is the eternal story where life and death face one another, or where life and death exist in close proximity. He looks upon the principal incidents of the film as transpiring on that frontier which separates life from death. Various tricks and subterfuges (*trucs*) were necessary in the creation of the film so that the thoughts of the poet (Orpheus and Cocteau) would be presented as something real, as truth, in fact.

Cocteau's first treatment of this theme was written in 1925, as the play *Orphée*. So many differences exist between the two works, it would be improper to consider the film an adaptation of the play. There is a horse in the play, which transmits messages and poems to Orphée. In the film, the horse has been replaced by the automobile of the princess. This princess is Death, or rather Orphée's death. The automobile of the princess is driven by Heurtebise, who in the play was window repairer and the guardian angel of Orphée and Eurydice. Heurtebise is now a chauffeur, and the radio of the auto transmits incoherent or enigmatic messages that fascinate Orphée. But this takes place before Orphée descends into hell, or, as it is called in the film, *la zone*. This is a no-man's land between life and death. It is the place composed of the memories of men and their habits. *La zone* may be another example of the illusion that time and space provide us with. It may be the coma, or the brief second separating life and death.

In the film itself, Heurtebise is defined as a young man

who is dead and who is in the service of Death or the princess. Orphée considers the princess omnipotent, but she tells him there are countless figures of Death, that carry out the orders of Death. Even she does not know who Death is. He lives nowhere. Some believe that he sleeps and that men are his dream—his bad dream. All the characters in the film, including the motorcyclists and the princess herself, are as far off from The Unknown as are we, who look upon ourselves as living.

But the actions of the princess, which create the drama, are free actions decided upon by herself. The theme of free will is important in *Orphée*. The princess dares to take the place of destiny when she plays the role of a woman in love with Orphée, whom she was supposed to watch over. Cocteau is careful to say that he does not know what her punishment will be.

Before his death, the artist and stage designer Christian Bérard had prepared models for the sets (*maquettes*). When the film was being shot, Cocteau was alone for this part of the work, but he and Bérard had talked about *la zone*, and had decided it should be simple and anti-Dantesque. The scenes were taken in the ruins of Saint-Cyr.

Where does poetry come from? To this question, the play *Orphée* of 1926 has a first answer: it comes from the depths of the self (*des profondeurs du moi*). The film *Orphée* gives a more complicated and less precise answer. Orphée receives the poems from the radio. Cégeste, the young poet who is dead, transmits them. But from where does he get them, we might ask. There is no answer in the film. Cocteau took them from Apollinaire and from his own book *Opéra*.

The plot or story of the film is as simple as a Greek tragedy, as *Antigone*, or as a Racine tragedy, *Bérénice*, for example. This would be one way of expressing it: the Death of the poet Orphée falls in love with him, and thereby repudiates the laws of earth and hell. She is punished by a tribunal, and then order returns. There is also a subsidiary subject or plot: the worldly destiny of the poet Orphée. Other poets are jealous of him and envy him. The Club of the Bacchantes hate him and prefer the new avant-garde poet Cégeste. We see him in his human relationship with his wife Eurydice. He is cruel to her because she understands nothing about poetry.

In both *Le Sang d'un poète* and *Orphée*, we see a series of deaths and rebirths concerning the poet. The problem remains: what is the source of a poem? It comes from my night, says Orphée of the play *(de ma nuit)*. It comes from somewhere else, says Orphée of the film: *un ailleurs où habite la mort*. It is this kind of aesthetic problem, as well as the photography, the adaptation of the myth, that caused almost a battle during the year 1950-51. France is famous for this kind of battle over a new dramatic work: *Le Cid, Andromaque, Hernani, Pelléas et Mélisande, Cyrano de Bergerac, Ubu Roi*.

This is the third work of Cocteau in which he studies the drama of the creator. *Orphée* of 1926, *Le Sang d'un poète* of 1932, *Orphée* of 1950. But for the first time he uses two poets: Orphée and Cégeste. In every way they are opposed to one another. Orphée (Jean Marais) is the national figure, the one who has received all honors. But Cégeste (Edouard Dermit) is the favorite of the young, of the avant-garde. He edits the magazine *Nudisme*, which publishes only white pages. Orphée calls this ridiculous *(c'est ridicule!)* but another writer replies: "Less ridiculous than if the pages were covered with ridiculous poems."

At the beginning of the film, in the café scene, we learn that Orphée's work is considered old-fashioned by the avant-garde. And later in the film there is a scene of outright hostility toward Orphée on the part of the public. At first Orphée scorned Cégeste because the younger poet's work contradicted his. And yet, after his meeting with the princess, Orphée received radio poems sent by Cégeste. He does not understand the poems, but their strangeness moves him deeply. By illuminating simultaneously the two poets, Cocteau emphasizes the drama of the creative artist by speaking of the avant-garde and the established poet.

When the tribunal in *la zone* questions Orphée on his profession, he answers: "I'm a poet."

The clerk says: "Your card says writer."

"It's almost the same thing."

"There is no almost here. What do you mean by poet?"

"To write without being a writer."

In the play, Orphée passes through a mirror to reach death or hell. In the film, *la zone* is that place beyond the mirrors. The character of the princess is the most human in the film. There is an admirable love scene between Orphée and the princess, between a mortal man and a dead woman, on the threshold of the beyond, of *la zone*. When at the end of the film she is in *la zone* waiting for the poet to come to her, she says to Cégeste: "It is the first time I have almost had an understanding of time. It must be a terrible thing for men to wait." *C'est la première fois que j'ai presque la notion du temps. Ce doit être affreux pour les hommes d'attendre.*

The understanding Cocteau brought to poetry throughout his career, in all the varied art forms he used, is perhaps his most important contribution. This was illustrated in *Le Sang d'un poète* and *Orphée*. *Le Testament d'Orphée*, Cocteau's final film, of 1960, is a conscious culmination of this search, an expression of his belief that the art of the movie (*la cinématographie*) is as much a vehicle for poetry as words or graphic art. Cocteau never adhered to one simple theory of poetry, to one coherent poetics. At times he looked upon poetry as something very private, as the expression of an intimate alchemy. At other times he looked upon it as something more objective, as an objective, as an object, an enigma, an escutcheon *(blason)* which can be used by a reader in terms of himself. According to this definition, a poem represents the poet by its style rather than by its subject matter.

In *Le Testament d'Orphée*, the young poet Cégeste takes the poet Cocteau away from the questions asked by members of the tribunal at the end of *Orphée*. Cégeste, the young poet who had died in the earlier film, had been left by Orphée in *la zone*. In the aesthetic sense, Cégeste is the poem, and when he asks Cocteau for an accounting, we realize the poet owes such an allegiance only to his poem. In this last film, Jean Cocteau plays his own role. He converts his own life into a legend. He converts it into the legend his life had already become.

At the same time Cocteau was shooting his film in 1959, a film of Vadim (a brilliant new film director) had been censured for immorality. Cocteau expressed the hope that his own film would be censured for imbecility: forbidden to all over sixteen *(interdit aux plus de seize ans)*.

Picasso was often with Cocteau during the making of *Le Testament d'Orphée*, and used to encourage him with such words as: "Your film will do what it wants to. Like my paintings. I begin them and then they paint themselves. They do as they wish. Your film will not obey you." Of the many remarks that Cocteau himself made about his film, one in particular summarizes his intention. Among the elements in the work, he listed: the quarries of white stone used as the

Cocteau in the film, *Le Testament d'Orphée,* 1960

principal setting, Edouard Dermit, the other actors, the music. All of that, Cocteau said, is the castle, and the film is the ghost in the castle.

Most of the film was made in Les Baux-de-Provence, a village in southern France. It is on a hill and seems made of white chalk. The entrance to Les Baux is called *le val d'enfer*, the valley of hell, because Dante once lived there and one legend claims it inspired certain scenes in the *Inferno*.

At the bottom of the hill, a large hotel has been built against the rock. This hotel, La Baumanière, has been used by such celebrities as Churchill, Onassis the Greek shipbuilder, Bernard Buffet the painter, Ali Kahn. During the weeks, in 1959, of serious work on *Le Testament d'Orphée*, this hotel was completely reserved for Jean Cocteau and the crew of technicians and the many friends and artists who contributed their time and talent, and who helped him to photograph the final testament of the poet.

When Cocteau first discovered this setting, some years before 1959, he realized that the white grottoes of Les Baux could be converted into a fantastic setting. He dreamed of making a film there of *Britannicus*, but this was never realized. On another occasion, when Jean-Paul Sartre asked him to make a film of *Les Mouches*, he considered using Les Baux. This project also was never realized.

For *Le Testament d'Orphée*, a committee was formed to help Cocteau and his producer Jean Thuilier. Among those whose help persevered during the long months of work on the film were André Malraux, the writer and minister, and Truffault, the young film director, famous for *Les Quatre Cents Coups*. Vadim, another film director of the *nouvelle vague*, brought several young people from nearby Saint-Tropez, to help decorate the film.

The large number of Cocteau's friends who have acting

parts, most of which are very small, makes Le Testament d'Orphée comparable to the triumph of Irène, the final tragedy of Voltaire when, after the performance, all the actors clustered about the bust of the writer on the stage, to pay homage to him, in 1778. Since Cocteau himself plays the poet in Le Testament, Jean Marais appears in the role of Oedipus. Three other characters from Orphée play their same roles: Maria Casarès as the princess, and François Périer as Heurtebise. They do not know, or pretend they do not know, who Cégeste is, the younger man played by Edouard Dermit. Dermit plays two roles: Cégeste the character and himself who is a painter and the adopted son of Cocteau. Cocteau also plays two parts: himself and the role of the poet. The three characters, Cégeste, the princess, and Heurtebise seem to come to Cocteau in Le Testament because of the mysterious bonds joining the creatures of an author's imagination with himself.

Other friends who appear briefly in this testament are: the actor Yul Brynner, who guards the entrance to hell, the French actor Daniel Gélin, the painter Picasso, the singer Aznavour, the matador Dominguin, the writer Françoise Sagan, gypsies (gitans) from Saintes-Maries-de-la-Mer, Mme Alec Weisweiller, in whose villa at Saint-Jean-Cap-Ferrat Cocteau lived several years. There is a scene in the film showing Mme Weisweiller in the garden of her villa.

Cocteau, at the age of seventy, is the principal actor in this film of which he is also hero, author, director. He was indefatigable during the shooting of the film and seemed to everyone remarkably agile and youthful. He refused to use a double and performed himself all the difficult scenes, including the dangerous scene where Minerva throws a spear at him.

The richness of the film is bewildering: horses in the Babylonian setting of Les Baux, gatemen of hell in tuxedos, with heads like Yul Brynner's, flowers that are torn and put together by fire, motorcycle policemen of death, Oedipus, his eyes gouged out, sphinxes, Minerva, masks of Anubis, death masks, a statue with three faces whose eyes are sea-shells and who is probably Tiresias the soothsayer, settings that resemble the interior of an Egyptian pyramid. This is the universe through which Jean Cocteau walks, accompanied by Cégeste who could easily be looked upon as an angel.

In one of the scenes, Heurtebise says that Cégeste is the name of the temple in Sicily. And the poet answers that it is also the young poet in his film *Orphée*. But it was first the name of one of Cocteau's angels in his early poem *L'Ange Heurtebise*. In the film's subtitle, which is heard at the end: *Ne me demandez pas pourquoi* ("Do not ask me why"), Cocteau says he is incapable of explaining why he filmed this adventure which does not adhere to the usual movie techniques.

The beginning of the film is taken in a film studio in Nice, studio 4 of La Victorine. The props used are those designed to create the atmosphere of an empty space, of quite literally a movie studio. Cocteau tries in this opening scene to create a farce in the style of Goldoni. It is a mix-up of space, time, and sound.

At the end of the film, Cocteau tricks two motorcycle policemen, two *motards*. After his disappearance, a sportscar from which we hear jazz scatters the identification papers of Cocteau, which on reaching the ground, become the flower he has tried to bring to life in order to offer it to Minerva, goddess of reason. This is the point where she refuses the flower and pierces him with her spear. Throughout such sequences, it is well to remember Cocteau's statement that he is not a maker of films in the ordinary sense (*je ne suis pas un cinéaste*). He calls himself a poet using the camera as a vehicle for the projection of dreams.

IX
THE POET
AS THEORIST
AND CHRONICLER

To write in any form would seem to have been for Cocteau an exercise in critical taste. When the topic was given him, or chosen by him, it would immediately turn into a means of excitement and stimulation. The discussion would begin at once and he would inevitably reach a new discovery of himself and formulate a new accomplishment of his mind. All of Cocteau's work can justifiably be called "a poetry of criticism," because in it he gives himself over without effort to the delights of judging, to the enjoyment of a game of ideas which forms the basis of criticism. Cocteau is one of those French writers—novelists, poets, dramatists—who are critics, and among the finest that France has produced, critics not only in their critical essays but also in their creative works: Baudelaire, Mallarmé, Gide, Valéry. In the realm of aesthetics, Cocteau's *Rappel à l'ordre* has its place beside Baudelaire's *Art romantique* and Gide's *Prétextes*. In the realm of ethics, Cocteau's *La Difficulté d'être* ranks easily with La Bruyère's *Caractères*, with Joubert, and with the best pages in Julien Green's *Journal*.

In the most natural way possible, a critical position is taken by Cocteau when he writes. His *Antigone*, for example, is a criticism of Sophocles; his *Plain-Chant* is a criticism of traditional love poetry; his *Secret professionnel* is a criticism of criticism. His method is always a simplification of some artform, of some artifice that needs to be recast. The measurements have to be changed, the exaggerations restricted, and the implications deepened. If the point of departure is common sense or something reasonable, Cocteau may well add to it a twist of singularity or of insolence. To a theme of innocence he may add a pose of studied indifference, of detachment. The slow tempo of wisdom will be speeded up, even indiscreetly. The treatise that normally would be heavy and cumbersome, Cocteau will compress into startling affirmations without proof, without research. He refuses to be commentator or exegete. He does not even tolerate the rational steps of his own mind. In real life he was a tireless speaker, but when he wrote, he was always laconic, cuttingly brief. He wrote in flashes and aphorisms. This was his style. He had learned to stop writing when he had articulated what he wanted to say.

In answering the question: What is style? Cocteau said on one occasion that for most people, it is a complicated way of saying very simple things, but that for him it is a very simple way of saying complicated things: *une façon très simple de dire des choses compliquées.* Cocteau understood the deep simplicity of commonplaces and trained his talent in restating them in new guises for a new age. He often conjugates old bits of wisdom of the race with well-worn commonplaces, so that together they appear as two opposing principles. His aphorisms are dramatic. They are often miniature plays destined to be seen on a stage by a public who expects some visible conflict. With words, Cocteau is a stage director carefully placing his actors in strategic positions.

Cocteau recapitulates many of the romantic views concerning the poet: he is an inspired figure, alone, aloof, outcast. But he believes poetry needs the full intelligence of this man. To reach Cocteau's ideal of very simple and very bare poetry, he has to use props and machines which are sometimes called tricks of witchcraft. To be pure despite all the traps of words and rhetoric demands the skill of a magician. His facile use of puns, in prose and verse alike, is one way of demonstrating the critic's skill in reducing words to a form capable of carrying a thought. His own name designates the "rooster early" *(coq tôt)* singing before daybreak.

The critic by profession as well as by nature is the analyst of a work, the interpreter of a work, and for this kind of writing he uses his memory, his thoughts concerning all the books he had known. Cocteau's attitude toward criticism is radically different from this. His memories are called into play, inevitably, but he is never the analyst of his memories or of a work of art. He is a spectator. Astonished, innocent, serious, he watches the spectacle of his memories and speaks of them as if they were performing for him an action of which he cannot tell the ending. There is no way of judging that which has no conclusion.

Rather than resolving riddles, Cocteau turned into the sphinx of his age. He writes as if he inhabits a zone where all is truth, where there is no need for argumentation, no need for weighing judgments, no need for even referring to disorder because the new order of the twentieth century had been sensed and proclaimed by Apollinaire in the early years. When Cocteau himself denounced the facile *bavardage* of his earliest writings, he began his own adventure with order, which he was to call "poetry" and which was an acceptance of some inner personal illumination. Others have called it, in referring to Cocteau, a mask, an affectation, a trick. It does often resemble a dangerous exhibitionism, a tightrope stunt, in full view of the spectators who watch hypnotized by the performance when there is every chance for catastrophe.

In the early years, in the twenties, the public watched Cocteau only when the fanfare was strident. They quickly turned away when each performance ended. Then during the years that immediately followed the Second World War, in the late forties and early fifties, after the death of Valéry, when Claudel and Gide published their correspondence, when Sartre and Camus were denouncing the world's absurdity, when Picasso began working in porcelain, the works of Jean Cocteau continued to appear. He was still there, and the new works, while fully recognizable, were reaching a fuller dimension of thoughtfulness and wisdom. His place had to be acknowledged with the appearance in 1946 of *La Difficulté d'être*, and, in 1952, of *Journal d'un inconnu*. These two books, of a critical nature, were not only the most profound of Cocteau's work, but took their place among the really significant books of the age.

In the refining of his method of writing, which is also his method of criticism, Cocteau acknowledged on several occasions his masters. In the final editing of a film Chaplin explained to Cocteau that he used to shake the tree so that only what was firmly attached to the branches would remain. Satie he used to call his schoolmaster, and Radiguet his examiner. Both of these men, one much older than Cocteau, and the other much younger, helped him to reach the swiftness and simplicity of his writing. They taught him how important it was to forget he was a poet and to allow the phenomenon of creation to take place without his realizing it.

The critic's method is identical with the poet's, in a fundamental sense for Cocteau. Whereas the more typical poet
tends to hide the object under the poetry, and the critic
tends to hide the subject of his criticism under the jargon
and the system of his criticism, Cocteau does the reverse: he
hides the poetry under the object, and he hides the method
of criticism under the subject of the criticism. It is sometimes
difficult to remember that under the arch-simplicity of one of
his poems, the major themes of love and death are present.
And likewise, it is not always apparent, on a first reading of a
paragraph of his criticism, that he is claiming for the powers
of art and morality more than is usually claimed in our day.
As a pharmacist mixes herbs to make a cure, as a painter
mixes colors to make a picture, so Cocteau mixes proper
names (Antigone, Oedipus) to make a play, and concepts to
reveal the hidden resources of the artists of his day.

Cocteau's first critical writing, *Le Coq et l'Arlequin*, was
published in 1918, in les éditions de la Sirène, which he had
founded with Blaise Cendrars. It is a kind of manifesto in
favor of the new music of Satie and Stravinsky, and an
attack on the music of Wagner and Debussy. The work,
written in brief aphoristic sentences, is fundamentally a
defense of *Parade*, and the aesthetics of simplicity in the
music of Erik Satie. It initiated a polemic between Cocteau
and Gide, which appeared in part on the pages of *La
Nouvelle Revue Française*, and it was widely discussed in the
cafés.

In his dedicatory letter to Georges Auric, Cocteau explains
that he admires the Harlequins of Cézanne and Picasso, but
he does not like Harlequin. Harlequin denies his master at
the crowing of the cock. He is a night cock who says "Cocteau" twice and lives on his own farm. After the vogue of
Wagner and Debussy, Satie taught the boldest lesson to his

age: the lesson of simplicity. The aesthetics of *Le Coq et l'Arlequin* is a series of formulas designed to reinforce this claim. *Satie enseigne la plus grande audace à notre époque: être simple.*

At this time, in an underground café *(une cave)* on the rue Huyghens, a medley of artists and society people crowded about every evening to hear the new music of *Les Six* (Georges Auric, Arthur Honegger, Darius Milhaud, Francis Poulenc, Germaine Taillefer, and Louis Durey), and to hear new poems of Cocteau, Apollinaire, Max Jacob, and Pierre Reverdy.

During the months when the Dada movement was showing its principal manifestations in Paris, Cocteau was publishing a series of articles in the newspaper *Paris-Midi* between March 31, 1919 and August 11. The majority of these pieces, ultimately published in book form under the title *Carte Blanche*, were devoted to extolling the new music and new poetry. The articles form the literary and artistic chronicle of the day, in which Cocteau discusses the "futurism" of Marinetti; the musical setting of Louis Durey to *Les Images à Crusoé* of Saint Léger-Léger (Saint-John Perse); an exhibit of paintings of Juan Gris, *un Espagnol qui habite Paris*; the histrionic art of Charlie Chaplin and Mistinguett; the key position of Satie in the new music *(Satie joue le rôle de poteau indicateur. La jeunesse consulte la flèche)*; the kind of dancing visible in *les bals musette*; a penetrating assessment of Max Jacob to whom, according to Cocteau, all the Paris artists and writers owe something *(nous lui devons tous quelque chose)*; the new exoticism realized by Blaise Cendrars in such a work as *La Prose du Transsibérien*, the intoxicated train, coming after the drunken boat *(Train saoûl après Le Bateau ivre)*.

In 1922, in company with Radiguet, at Le Piquet, on the

bay of Arcachon, Cocteau wrote *Le Secret professionnel,* one of the significant critical-theoretical texts of the period. It is a poetics, a treatise on the need for simplicity in the arts of poetry and the theatre. The example of Radiguet's kind of writing and of Radiguet's theory were unquestionably incorporated in *Le Secret professionnel.* Cocteau is less concerned with technical problems of aesthetics than with the moral values involved in the writing of poetry. The notion of poetry involves a commitment of the poet's entire being. At the beginning of the essay, Flaubert is discussed as the type of writer who holds his gun for a long time in the position of firing, and who is not concerned with the target. Cocteau claims that the so-called realistic tableaux of Flaubert are far from reality. Cocteau distrusts a learned art of verbal combinations and all the noble attitudes of poets when they speak of revolt and blasphemy. Whenever anarchy becomes official or whenever suffering is presented as triumphant, Cocteau is wary.

He is searching for another principle in art and he gives to this principle the name *angelism.* Several terms are used for its definition, and they are presented with their opposites, so that one cancels out the other: disinterestedness and egoism, pity and cruelty, a liking for earthly pleasures and a scorn for them. By this coupling of contradictions, the divine is discovered in a human being, and such a being, in his naive amorality, will appear suspect to most. By the title "professional secret," Cocteau is saying that a poet uses a certain number of secrets in his poetry, and the art of poetry is such that these secrets are not revealed, that the poet is not dispossessed of them. He practices with them, because poetry is more profoundly a state of being than merely an art of writing.

Cocteau denounces the pessimism and the spirit of destructiveness he finds in romanticism and in the romantic's taste for ruins. On defining the signs of angelism he finds in modern poetry, he names Rimbaud the leading exponent, who combines the extremes of disinterestedness and egoism: *Jusqu'à nouvel ordre, Arthur Rimbaud reste le type de l'ange sur terre.* A passage in the center of the essay defines poetry in a way closely allied to the surrealist method. It is poetry seen in its role of revealer, of unveiler, when abruptly it is able to name a familiar object that had been accepted mechanically and that is seen in a new light dispelling the torpor with which it is usually surrounded. This is for Cocteau the creation of poetry. *Elle dévoile, dans toute la force du terme.*

Cocteau claims he has no knowledge about poetry's power to unite man with religion or separate him from it. He comments on Claudel's famous sentence in his preface to the works of Rimbaud which calls the poet a mystic in a barbaric state: *Rimbaud était un mystique à l'état sauvage.* This he accepts: that poetry is a religious spirit outside of any specific religion. What does the poet believe? questions Cocteau. He believes everything. Skepticism is a poor conductor for poetry, and that is why France, as a country, according to Cocteau, is not very receptive to poetry. *C'est pourquoi la poésie touche peu en France, pays malin.*

In a lecture given at the Collège de France, on May 3, 1923, Cocteau pays special homage to those artists he calls his masters. *D'un ordre considéré comme une anarchie* is in many ways the writer's self-evaluation, an analysis of his previous work, of the changes that had taken place in his tastes, and of his admiration for several contemporary artists. He names Rimbaud, Mallarmé, and Lautréamont as the immediate precursors of his generation. The symbol of night, so often associated with their work, Cocteau claims is a false type of darkness (*ténèbres fausses*). Their "night" is so concentrated that it appears finally with the luminosity of a diamond.

He names quite simply the two men to whom he owes the most: *Je cite mes maîtres: Erik Satie et Picasso*. The composer and the painter taught Cocteau the significant discipline of freedom. When accused of constantly changing their style, of not knowing where they were going, Satie and Picasso would reply that all great artists are amateurs. The birth of a very clear, very simple work is usually not recognized. Cocteau and those writers just slightly older than himself, such as Max Jacob and Apollinaire, were hostile to the inflated art of the nineteenth century. They were unwilling to repeat the rhetorical devices of Rimbaud, Mallarmé, and Lautréamont. The new writers of 1920: Jacob, Cocteau, Paul Morand; and the new composers: Milhaud, Auric, and Satie, disliked what Cocteau called in his lecture "family dinners" or new artistic schools. *Haïssons les dîners de famille, les systèmes*. Picasso is not a cubist, he would say. And Mallarmé was not a Mallarmist. Any preconceived notion about poetry and music is grotesque.

In 1928, these separate essays were collected by Cocteau into one volume which he called *Le Rappel à l'ordre*. He included three short texts: *Visites à Maurice Barrès*, an account of his meetings with Barrès during the war; *Autour de "Thomas l'imposteur"*, a critique of his novel which had appeared in *Les Nouvelles Littéraires*, October 27, 1923, in which he analyzes the *anti-bizarrerie* of his work; and *Picasso*, an important essay on the painter, which had first appeared in 1923. In his analysis of the qualities of economy and clairvoyance in Picasso's art, Cocteau restates his aesthetic position that dominates all the writings collected in *Le Rappel à l'ordre*. It is a midway position, classical in its opposition to the verbal anarchy of a Rimbaud and Jarry, and avant-garde in its design to shock and startle spectators and readers. The aesthetics of *Le Coq et l'Arlequin* is a crusade against the obscurity, the "fuzziness" of certain nineteenth-century artists, against an over-facile use of the tradition of the *poètes maudits*. The problems of talent and genius are studied as values in *Le Rappel à l'ordre*. These early essays are exercises in style and articulation of thought, as well as statements of belief of an apprentice who had rapidly become professional. The themes of the essays are so intertwined one with the other that it is difficult to follow in them an "order" in the usual sense of the word. The thesis of the work might be defined as the danger of ornamentation; for a writer, the danger of any development or prolongation once the *trouvaille* is discovered. One striking, swift metaphor is sufficient to bear the burden of a thought. Cocteau's own art, of course, best illustrates such a thesis.

The moral importance of Cocteau's work, and especially of his critical writing, was first revealed in *Lettre à Jacques Maritain*. This was published in 1926 immediately after three theatrical works: *Orphée* and the two adaptations of *Antigone* and *Roméo et Juliette*. The friendship of Maritain was a consolation for Cocteau at a very difficult and even tragic moment in his life. It helped to initiate not a new attitude toward art, but a more carefully defined attitude toward art.

Lettre à Maritain is a summary of many matters in Cocteau's life and career, of subjects he had discussed in earlier writings and which now are reviewed and analyzed in the light of his friendship with Jacques Maritain and Père Charles, the priest he had met at Maritain's house in Meudon. It had become clear to him that the fundamental seriousness of art has a religious explanation. He had always been distrustful of miracles and mysticism. The aesthetics of his art, or at least aspects of this aesthetics appeared to have religious connotations, and terms he had always used had suddenly taken on a purer meaning. He writes of "the algebra of love in what remains of our faith" and the "melody of silence in the Virgin."

The basic method used in his art now seems to be sincerity, an almost religious need to tell everything, to expose everything, to live naked. He speaks of seven friends who had been taken from him by death (Garros and Radiguet were among them) and he now sees these losses in a different way. God had not really taken these young people away. He had simply put costumes on angels. The image of "gloves of heaven" *(gants du ciel)* is here used by Cocteau to define the kind of artist he considers Raymond Radiguet. To touch us without soiling itself, Heaven puts on gloves. When Heaven takes its hand out of the glove, death occurs. *Lorsque le ciel ôte sa main, c'est la mort.*

The *Lettre* contains personal confidences, such as the effect of Père Charles on Cocteau, a brief history of the development of the arts in Paris between 1918 and 1923, and several aphorisms on art and specific artists which recapitulate and sometimes clarify earlier formulas of Cocteau. He emphasizes the belief that the new language of poetry must be liberated from the style of Rimbaud and the "superstitions" of Maldoror. If Cocteau is in the process of learning that art is religious, he is also determined to point out the danger of religious art.

The image of the tightrope had been used by Cocteau to describe his form of classicism and he revives it in *Lettre à Maritain* in order to point out the relationship between his aesthetics of simplicity and Catholicism. Both the aesthetics and the religion are his own. It is incorrect to speak of "conversion" in Cocteau's case. *La corde raide me mène au catholicisme; c'est-à-dire chez moi; il est donc faux de parler de conversion.*

The volume *Opium*, with the subtitle, *journal d'une désintoxication*, was published in 1930 with several drawings by Cocteau. It is quite literally a diary written and drawn by Cocteau in the clinic of Saint Cloud, between December 1928 and April 1929, while he was being treated for an addiction to opium. Some notations were added to the galley proofs in 1930. The phases of the cure are described as well as the effects of the use of the drug. Opium had quite literally excluded Cocteau from its rites.

The diary of the cure is almost the pretext for commentary on many other subjects, including some of Cocteau's own books: *Les Enfants terribles*, for example, whose subject forced itself on him while he was at the clinic, and which he wrote during three weeks. He claims the book wrote itself and that he was the scribe. The physical suffering endured by Cocteau during the treatment is graphically transcribed in the drawings far more than it is described in the text. The style of the writing is as concise as ever and the thoughts are as aphoristically expressed as always. Cocteau's writing is always a form of *ascesis*, but because of the subject matter of *Opium*, it is here blatantly a rite of purification, a cure of the body and spirit. He is not concerned with describing a sensory paradise, but with measuring the degree of lucidity his mind had reached. The brief notations in *Opium*, which are often observations of reality and aesthetic principles and moral comments, will be expanded into paragraphs and chapters in subsequent volumes, in two especially: *La Diffi-*

culté d'être and *Journal d'un inconnu*. The moralist in Cocteau, in 1929, is still tentative. He is still close to the effort he made to escape from himself and from his sufferings.

The man who writes and who suffers as he writes, as in *Opium*, is undertaking the task of going against himself. He is instituting a lawsuit against opium because he claims he does not belong to it. Jean Cocteau is free and intends to remain so. No one world, no one artificial paradise can hold him. No one adventure is exclusive or definitive. The writing of *Opium* was one of the means of curing himself of the addiction. By writing about the art of writing, and the agility of the human spirit, and the essence of art, Cocteau moved out of the immediate past which had threatened to hold him down, and into a period of marked fertility.

The volume *Essai de critique indirecte*, published in 1932, is in two parts, of which the first, *Le mystère laïc*, had appeared in 1928, and of which the second, *Des beaux-arts considérés comme un assassinat*, is concerned with the paintings of Giorgio di Chirico. But every announced subject is a pretext for other subjects, for other diversions. By reflecting on one object foreign to one's mind, one discovers the realities and the passions of one's mind. The "secular mystery" in *le mystère laïc* is that art which is foreign to religious dogma, but it turns out that *le mystère laïc* is essentially spiritual.

Essai de critique indirecte is a confirmation, ten years later, of the aesthetics of *Le Rappel de l'ordre*, but the tone of the book and the atmosphere around it have changed. The form of the aphorisms is more tormented, more anguished. The "assassination" in the title of the second essay refers to a principle allied to the catharsis of Aristotle. Every work of art is the quelling or the death of an original impulse in the artist. But his genius, if that is what he has, will work for new victims to bring about his rebirth.

To the ethical in a work of art, Cocteau ascribes a higher place than to the purely aesthetic. The artist cannot renew his work without living dangerously and hence calling forth slander. *J'estime que l'art reflète la morale et qu'on ne peut se renouveler sans mener une vie dangereuse et donnant prise à la médisance.* This point separates Cocteau from Maritain, who believes art to be a dangerous game, a caricature of creation, and who believes morality stable.

This age is one of "mystery," acccording to Cocteau, and the poet is the one on whom the unknown falls. More forcibly than in earlier writings Cocteau calls poetry a calamity of birth *(une calamité de naissance)*. A great artist is inhuman, and when he speaks, what he says is upsetting to his age. A poem is a closed world totally hostile to the casual visitor. Cocteau looks on the paintings of Chirico in the same way. The streets in the paintings do not invite the spectators. It is as if they bore the sign *one way*.

More than being a commentary on the art of Chirico, *Le mystère laïc* is a poetics, or at least Cocteau's writing which comes closest to being a poetics. Chirico chooses familiar objects for his paintings, but places them in such unusual juxtapositions that they translate, with the precision of poetry *(la poésie, c'est l'exactitude)*, the spiritual anguish of man, the darkness of his inner life. Pervading *l'essai* is a deeper sense of anxiety than in other writings of Cocteau. In losing the sense of mystery, modern man has upset the economy of the world. In today's world everything has to be explained. The police question and observe from the outside all the family secrets. That is why everything in the paintings of Chirico (and everything in the poems of Jacob and Cocteau): walls, arcades, shadows, equestrian statues, an egg placed in a desert, a rubber glove hanging near a plaster head, will seem suspect.

Cocteau argues that every masterpiece is made up of mysteries, of disguised confessions, calculations, puns. He cites Da Vinci and Watteau, whose secrets are carefully concealed: *un Léonard, un Watteau, deux cachottiers connus*. Chirico is the decorator of theatrical peripeteia. Only a small number of his spectators know what they are looking at.

The articles included in *Portraits-souvenir* (1900-1914) were written at the beginning of 1935 for the Saturday edition of *Le Figaro*, and they were intended to reveal the personal life of Cocteau and the artistic life of Paris between 1900 and 1914. The memories narrated are of childhood and adolescence. They center on the theatre, on friendships, on early experiences of the heart and mind. The twenty-six articles are brilliantly evocative. They are notes for an autobiography, selected memories that describe Paris at the turn of the century and that explain elements of Cocteau's portrait: the social world from which he came, his early attachment to the theatre, his interest in music, the importance of Dargelos in his life, his friendship with Rilke, with Christian Bérard, and the place in his memories of Villefranche and the Hôtel Welcome.

The articles resemble drawings from memory. Despite the number of years that have elapsed between the time of the activities and the writing of *Portraits-souvenir*, there is no sadness in the evocation. Cocteau appears as he must have appeared to many of those described in the book, as a Prince Charming. Effortlessly, as if by magic, the past is brought back. The circus, the school friends, the apparition of Mistinguett on the stage, the portraits of Catulle Mendès and Rostand, and especially the study of Anna de Noailles are clear transcriptions of the past into the present. Cocteau has the skill of enlarging what he wants to enlarge, but without deforming. Each scene has its own value, and a place in the background of the writer.

Portraits-souvenir was a voyage into the past, to certain cherished landscapes of the past, and *Mon premier voyage (Tour du monde en 80 jours)*, of 1936, is the account of a real journey, undertaken as a wager with the newspaper *Paris-Soir*. Cocteau left on March 28, 1936, and returned to Paris, June 17, after following the itinerary of Philéas Fogg, the character of Jules Verne. Cocteau adhered to the traditions of journalism in the swiftness with which he narrated his voyage, in the directness of his observations. André Gide, an accomplished traveler, had once accused Cocteau of not being able to observe the exterior world and describe it. *Mon premier voyage* is dedicated to Gide, and is a denial of the accusation. On the third page of his notebook, Cocteau acknowledges that he has been wandering through centuries not inscribed on maps and that from these worlds without atlas, he had brought back experiences that had not always pleased his readers. He had colonized unknown regions. And now he was ready to rest and wander over real land and take railroads and boats like everyone else. He compared the road he took to a serpent entwined around the globe. The head and the tail were in Paris.

If the book is a faithful mirror of things seen, it is also a mirror of the traveler in Rome, the heavy city *(ville lourde)*; on the Acropolis; in a café in Alexandria; before the sphinx; in Singapore; at a meeting with Charlie Chaplin on May 11 *(le miracle charmant de ce voyage)* on the boat between Hong-Kong and Shanghai. This chance encounter with Chaplin and Paulette Goddard gave Cocteau the greatest joy of the voyage. He did not speak English, and Chaplin spoke no French. Yet they spoke effortlessly. *Je ne parle pas anglais.*

Chaplin ne parle pas français. Et nous parlons sans le moindre effort. Chaplin called himself the most exposed man in the world because he works in the street. "The aesthetics of the kick in the behind. . . . And now I am beginning to receive it."

In New York, Cocteau observed the Lindy Hop in Harlem, listened to swing music, watched a performance of *Macbeth* played by Negro actors, visited Coney Island. Despite the speed of the journey, and the constantly changing scenes, *Mon premier voyage* does not have a surface brilliance. The commentaries are on significant representative details, on the enigmas of civilizations, on secrets of races and customs. The moral reflection always accompanies the description. The principal observed in *Essai de critique indirecte* is applied to the living in *Mon premier voyage*.

Maalesh, journal d'une tournée de théâtre, of 1949, is another kind of diary, begun on February 20, 1949, at the death of Christian Bérard. On the sixth of March, Cocteau left France by plane, with a company of twenty-two actors to put on a series of plays in Cairo, Alexandria, Istanbul, and Ankara. Among the actors were Yvonne de Bray, Jean Marais, Gabrielle Dorziat, Tania Balachova. They performed three plays of Cocteau: *La Machine infernale, Les Monstres sacrés,* and *Les Parents terribles.* The repertory also included *Britannicus* of Racine, *Huis clos* of Sartre, *Léocadia* of Anouilh, and a Feydeau play: *Léonie est en avance.* In his journal, Cocteau notes his impression of places, of people he encounters, of the performances of his actors, of the audiences who come to see the plays, of his cohabitation with the actors. He lectures often as a cultural ambassador from France. The diary narrates three months of wanderings in Egypt, Turkey, and Greece. Cocteau describes work in the theatre, official receptions, physical fatigue. Some of the passages concerning Egypt and Greece are developments of notes first taken in *Mon premier voyage*. Temples and tombs are sites where Cocteau feels especially in accord with the past. The work of excavators and achaeologists revealing settings for extraordinary spectacles of the past is curiously related to the performances of the French actors whom Cocteau was guiding. Life in the present with its activities, schedules, and risks is not more intense than life in the past of Istanbul, when it is evoked by Cocteau.

Even more than the journal of his voyage around the world and the journal of the theatrical tour of Maalesh, Cocteau's journal of his film, *La Belle et la bête*, describes his exceptional capacity for work, his will to overcome all the obstacles that are concomitant with work in the theatre and with the production of films. *La Belle et la bête, journal d'un film*, of 1946, is the account of the shooting of the film in 1945, where the endless technical problems are analyzed as they arose each day, and all the intimate reactions of Cocteau to these problems and to the idea of the film as a whole. Work devoured Cocteau to such an extent that he appeared to use it as a means of escape from the pain of living. He welcomed the purely manual aspect of film making in order to move out from the fearsome void of a life that had no physically exhausting exercise. The skin disease from which Cocteau suffered during the film production is analyzed as carefully as the labor on the film. The physical pain is not unrelated to the technical labor of the film shooting. He struggled to keep alive as he struggled to create the film.

No one term is adequate to describe the type of essay found in *La Difficulté d'être*, a collection of brief essays on moral and aesthetic themes. There are passages of confession in this volume of 1947, where Cocteau speaks intimately to his reader; there are portraits of friends and important celeb-

rities who had been carefully observed by Cocteau; there are
reminiscences of events and encounters; and there are, more
numerous than in other volumes, reflections on moral issues
which give to the volume as a whole an unusual gravity. *La
Difficulté d'être* seems almost to be a final communication to
all those interested in the career of Cocteau, an attempt to
justify a life that had appeared enigmatic and even scandal-
ous. It is the analysis of a man's mind when he wants to share
the best of his thought with his friends.

The title comes from Fontenelle who, almost one hundred
years old and close to death, said to his physician who had
just asked him how he felt: "I feel well, but I do feel some
difficulty in being." *(Bien. J'éprouve seulement une certaine
difficulté d'être.)* The repertory of all of Cocteau's themes is
here in this book, but they are more profoundly articulated,
as if death were felt to be imminent, as if this moment were
the last chance to mirror himself, to consider his varied
activities, his rich friendships, his obsessions, and the problems that no man can solve but which form a persistent part
of life, and which, when all is said, when the end is near, may
be seen to be extraordinary privileges.

The portraits are additions to some included in earlier
books: Radiguet, Nijinsky, and Diaghileff. As an aesthetician
he speaks of beauty, of the theatre, of words, and of readings
(De la beauté, Du théâtre, Des mots, De la lecture). There
are familiar essays about himself and about places where he
lived: *De mon enfance, Du travail et de la légende, De mon
physique, De mes évasions, De la France, Des maisons
hantées, Du Palais-Royal.* But the most precious essays of the
book are those in which Cocteau writes as a moralist, in
which the seriousness and originality of his thought are
expressed: *De l'amitié, De la douleur, De la mort, De la
frivolité, Du gouvernement de l'âme, Du rire, De la jeunesse,
Des moeurs, De la responsabilité.*

Cocteau reaches on these pages a fuller dimension of chronicler of his age because the portraits and the landscapes and the anecdotes are all utilized, not for the purpose of dazzling or amusing, but for the purpose of saying what should be preserved of a man's thoughts and memories, of putting into some kind of order the multiple difficulties of life. These can be expressed, but Cocteau knew as he wrote them that the difficulty of being cannot be expressed, cannot be put into that order which a page of writing represents.

The seriousness of *La Difficulté d'être* is continued in some of the pages of two other books: *Lettre aux Américains* of 1949, and *Journal d'un inconnu* of 1953. After spending twenty days in New York, where he helped direct the rehearsals of the Broadway production of *The Two-headed Eagle*, Cocteau wrote out, in the airplane taking him back to Paris, his impressions of America. He enumerated the paradoxes of New York: the desire to shock and the fear of shocking, the scorn of the theatre producer for the public he serves, the mysterious ways of Hollywood that had victimized Garbo and Chaplin. The success of *Le Sang d'un poète* in New York movie houses provoked commentaries which form an exegesis of the film, and corrections on various errors of interpretation. The film remains an enigma to Cocteau himself, but he would say that most of our actions are enigmatic. Cocteau was touched that his name was so well known to Americans (Harvard offered him a lectureship for a year), but he realized that Americans were not familiar with his books, and that an acquaintanceship with his books would bewilder and worry them.

In his *Lettre*, Cocteau quotes a passage from one of Baudelaire's essays on Poe in which the French poet defends the decadence of Europe. An American critic had once used the word "juggler" to humiliate Poe, and Baudelaire points out that he used the word in order to praise the noblest kind of poet. The word "clown" or "juggler" designates the ease with which a poet or thinker disguises the labor behind the finished work. As examples of masters of this art of juggling, Cocteau names Picasso, Eluard, Breton, Sartre, and Genet. He reminds Americans that those poets who have brought the greatest honor and prestige to France are men who had been pursued by the police: Villon, Baudelaire, Rimbaud, Nerval, Verlaine. We could add to the list the name of the poet Cocteau who continued to write out his thoughts during the night flight from New York to Paris, the figure of a free man, in the midst of that solitude which freedom requires, outside of all literary movements and churches and political parties. He had always written from some unlikely spot of solitude, such as an airplane in flight, and usually on the subject of freedom, and addressing his words to those who search for freedom.

Journal d'un inconnu, of 1953, is a group of essays which analyze familiar Cocteau themes, such as the essence of poetry *(De l'invisibilité)* and offer documentation on important events in Cocteau's life: the quarrel with François Mauriac, for example, over *Bacchus*; his complicated relationship with Gide, with Claude Mauriac, and with Maurice Sachs; the genesis of his poem *L'Ange Heurtebise*; the production of *Oedipus-Rex* in 1952.

Some of the most striking pages in *Journal d'un inconnu* were inspired by a new friend of Cocteau, the scientist René Bertrand, and his book *L'Univers cette unité*. In reading this scientific book, Cocteau had discovered confirmations for personal intuitions concerning phenomena of space and time which he claims are revealed to the poet through his own clairvoyance. The essay called *Des distances* is on this theme in which Cocteau combats man's tendency toward pessimism when he becomes aware of the prison of time and space.

"Celebrated but unknown": these two words are used by Cocteau to describe his position in the world. *Je suis sans doute le poète le plus inconnu et le plus célèbre.* The visible part of his being is made up of false legends, but this protects the invisible part and permits him to attack conformity of thinking and behavior. "Attack" is too strong a verb to use, because Cocteau is never aggressive. His action is not combat, but rather it is an effort to project light on what is vital, on what is truth for him.

The theme of invisibility and visibility occurs in Cocteau's text on Gide, *Gide vivant,* in which he defines Gide by his desire to be visible, to be a visible mystery, a visible enigma. The form of this text: questions asked Cocteau by Colin-Simard after Gide's death, followed by answers, forced Cocteau to explain his thought more deliberately, more methodically than he would have done in the ordinary form of an essay. The differences between the two men, in temperament, in ways of living, in methods of writing, and the fundamental differences in their work, make of this text a revealing document on the artist in a general sense, and on specific aspects of modern French literature. The text was published in 1952, soon after it was written, and republished in 1959 in *Poésie Critique I.*

Throughout his long life, Gide had made himself so visible by his habits of confession, his self-analysis, the detailed revelations of his thought and action, that after his death the critic-archaeologists found little to excavate. There were no surprises left. But, according to Cocteau, Gide always added a Voltairian skepticism, a Voltairian malice, to the Rousseau type of confession.

A curious form of jealousy, almost childlike in quality, estranged the two men at various times. Cocteau believed that Gide's real drama came from not being a poet. And yet there were moments of friendship and attentiveness. Gide, for example, greatly admired *Thomas l'imposteur* and *Le Secret professionnel*. But everything separated the two men: their temperaments and their books. Cocteau disliked the legends that had grown up about him and which on the whole were false. But Gide protected and encouraged his. Cocteau claimed that Gide had constructed his own labyrinth and enjoyed walking in it. But he never relinquished the thread which he held firmly in his hand. The gravity and seriousness of Gide are opposed to the nimbleness and wit of Jean Cocteau.

Each in his own way was a preacher of doctrines and each attracted a youthful audience. There are relationships between some of their works: the character Thomas in *Thomas l'imposteur* belongs to the same race as Lafcadio in *Les Caves du Vatican*. The world of *Les Parents terribles* bears some resemblance with that of *Les Faux-Monnayeurs*. Major differences between the two writers are visible in their personal writings: in the *Journal* of Gide, so conscientious in its analysis of impressions and events and readings, and Cocteau's two books of essays: *La Difficulté d'être* and *Journal d'un inconnu*, where memories are reduced to aphoristic interpretations and events are used as imaginary stories for moral and aesthetic principles. Circumstantial reporting becomes for Gide a means of self-exploration, whereas for Cocteau it is inevitably turned into an impersonally phrased intuition concerning the ways in which man lives and thinks and works.

Whereas Gide analyzes the habits of society that prevent man from reaching sincerity, Cocteau pays little heed to such matters in order to describe man as a solitary being moving about in the universe, a human solitude intent on stalking the invisible in himself and outside of himself, intent on sketching and articulating what comes to him from the perspective of dreams.

For Gide, the word "morality" preserves its classical meaning and hence designates the behavior of a man in society, the behavior of a man in terms of his fellow man. But for Cocteau, who also uses the word, it has a more vague meaning. It is a way of appearing or being in the world. It is the natural elegance of a man's soul. It is a form of secular grace bestowed on the *enfants terribles* of this world who are innocent and frail because they do not connive with the social forces. When writers are poets, in the Cocteau sense, they possess this morality and they acquire instinctivly the genius for solitude. Performers too, whether they be acrobats or tragediennes, are *monstres sacrés* for Cocteau when they inhabit the world of the invisible as much as they remain within the implacable demanding world of the visible.

The faculty of judging the actions of men is concomitant with the moral system as evolved by society. Man may be directed by other forces, such as the world of sleep, the virtues of childhood, the abiding power of friendship. These form, for Cocteau, not a system of values, but experiences based upon a spontaneous kind of inspiration. Cocteau was never able to bear ill-feeling toward anyone. As soon as a man seemed to be his enemy—Maurice Sachs or Gide or Mauriac —his whole way of living urged him to turn animosity or irritation into love and appreciation. A mere list of the various friends he helped is a moral commentary in itself: Cendrars, Maritain, Apollinaire, Satie, Genet.

He once called Picasso a Harlequin from Port-Royal, and he himself was a philosophical Harlequin who, whenever the performance of the play or the circus act was over, showed the audience the wings and the backstage, where the stage hands were taking down the set and putting away the props.

It is not difficult to praise striking details throughout the entire work of Cocteau, but it is more difficult to discover and explain the unifying force of inspiration, the bond that joins so many varied works. The nobility of his heart, a politeness associated with the manners of royalty, a generosity of spirit, are the first elements that will help define his genius. The solitude of the artist in Cocteau was always maintained, and perhaps for that very reason, as compensation. He gave of himself unstintingly in conversation, in help, in attentiveness, in friendship, to those who approached him.

When friendships became too involved with his work, whenever they threatened to become an obstacle to his work, he moved away from them, but not in order to eliminate friendships. As a very young man, he was flattered by the attention paid to him by such celebrities as Anna de Noailles and Maurice Barrès. But he did withdraw from the circle of such friends. A few years later, Cocteau was the friend of most of the leading surrealists, but he did not hesitate to leave them when he felt it important for him to write in accordance with a classical form of poetry. The same thing occurred at Meudon with the group of friends he met at the home of Jacques and Raïssa Maritain. The speed with which he worked and created was his own tempo, a necessity of his temperament, a need of his nature. He was an artisan as well as an artist and quite simply assumed responsibility of the labor involved in theatrical and film productions. He directed everyone with the passion of his spirit, convinced that even the most popular audiences would be touched by his art. The decoration of the Villefranche chapel was hard work done on scaffoldings where in graphic art he represented Saint Peter surrounded by a world of fishermen and which today is visited by all the tourists on the Riviera. The early advice given by Serge de Diaghileff: *étonne-moi*, was followed to the letter during the next quarter of a century during which each new work was the result of some comparable solicitation.

In his critical essays, as well as in his poems and films, Jean Cocteau sought to give back to the word "poetry" its literal meaning. He attempted to prove that poetry is never mere imitation but creation. All true creators: writers, sculptors, musicians, painters, are poets in the sense that a work of art is not an object in which a thought is fixed forever. It is comparable to the organism whose function is to give to the world a limitless number of meanings. Because of these meanings, destined to be revived each generation, Orpheus remains in the world. *Je reste avec vous* are the words engraved on the tombstone in the chapel of Saint-Blaise-des-Simples in Milly.

X
PICASSO'S ROLE
IN COCTEAU'S ART

Pablo Picasso is one of those artists—and he is perhaps more so than any other—who have shaped the modern sensibility. He and a few of his poet friends have altered our way of seeing and comprehending the world, and even our way of living. Around Picasso and around the contact which was established between him and men like Guillaume Apollinaire and Max Jacob at first, and later Jean Cocteau and Paul Eluard, there existed a veritable debauchery of artistic plots and fantasies and experimentations.

As almost always at the initial stage of such discoveries, a farcical atmosphere pervaded the intellectual and artistic fashions promulgated by Picasso and his friends. This tone of farce, of playfulness, is precisely what the general public detests the most in poetic movements. Cubism, fauvism, Negro art, dadaism, surrealism, the taste for serialized novels (*romans feuilletons*), and the theatre of the absurd, all emerged from an ambiency of jollification and mystification.

Picasso himself has always been reticent about speaking of himself and his work. The poets, among whom Cocteau holds first place, have not been reticent in analyzing the aesthetics of Picasso. What is known about the man Picasso, is due in large part to the writings of the poets. The role which Apollinaire and Cocteau have played for Picasso was formerly played by Baudelaire for Daumier and Delacroix and Constantin Guys. When Apollinaire spoke, he represented the group of poets and artists surrounding Picasso between 1903 and 1914, a group referred to now as *la bande à Picasso*. They were impoverished, but they heeded Apollinaire's firm word of counsel to love their century and to look upon the twentieth as far more exciting than the nineteenth. *Il faut aimer son époque. Notre 20e siècle est bien plus passionnant que le 19e.*

In the early years of the century Picasso's studio, at 13, rue Ravignan, in Montmartre, was the center for a group of artists and writers who shared poverty and ambitions. Apollinaire, Picasso, André Salmon, and Max Jacob formed a unified group destined to revolutionize arts and letters in France. Picasso was first proclaimed a master by the poets. The elf-like, ironic charm of Max Jacob bears affinities with Cocteau's art. Max possessed something of the prodigious virtuosity of Cocteau.

Picasso, Apollinaire, and Jacob were approximately the same age. At the beginning of their careers, when they were friends for the first time, they lived through years of poverty when they worried over the same preoccupations and the same kinds of ambition. Picasso's friendship with Jean Cocteau came a bit later and lasted longer, because it lasted until Cocteau's death in 1963. Cocteau often said that his meeting with Picasso was the most important of his life. The *Ode à Pablo Picasso* and the essay on the painter, one of the texts included in *Le Rappel à l'ordre*, as well as the many allusions scattered throughout the work, prove the influence, or rather the singular presence of Picasso in the thought and the aesthetic preoccupations of Jean Cocteau.

From the time of the First World War, about 1916, when he first met Picasso, Cocteau's activity continued unremittingly in all domains. Especially during the twenties and thirties, a prodigiously fertile period in French culture, Cocteau participated in a very intense artistic life in the capital. If his name became known to a wide public, he himself was understood by very few. Among those few, Pablo Picasso counted in a special way.

Picasso and Max Jacob understood better than others Cocteau's personal drama, which was often disguised by the exterior spectacle of his life. This impression is confirmed by these few lines of an unpublished letter of Max Jacob about Cocteau.

> We can never do enough to remove Jean's name from Paris society where he is so badly understood. Jean has the misfortune of being a man of wit. Some do not forgive him for this, and others pretend to find his wit his only charm. The truth is that his wit is always dazzling and conceals the other good attributes of the man. People are delighted to use this dazzling wit to conceal Jean's virtues, talents and gifts. . . . We must speak the truth. The truth is that Jean is a very great poet and, as I see it, the only poet we have had since Apollinaire's death. . . .

Picasso always admired the boldness with which Cocteau carried out his experimentations. The private asceticism by which Cocteau lived made of him a free man in the fullest sense of the word. The freedom he exemplified involving a life of considerable solitude, it provoked that "difficulty of being" which Cocteau described in his most profound book. It explains also the constant presence of death in his work.

His understanding of death, his impatient desire not to be late with himself, his fear of losing a single instant, explain at least to some degree Cocteau's fecundity and his prodigious vitality.

One day, soon after his first meeting with Picasso, Cocteau proposed to the painter to create a ballet for Serge de Diaghileff. This was to be *Parade*. We are in 1916. The eminent impresario of *Les Ballets Russes* took with him to Rome all of the collaborators in the work except Erik Satie, who refused to leave Paris. Cocteau was in charge of the score and the book. Picasso constructed the models for the stage set. Cocteau invented a kind of choreography. Feverishly they rehearsed in Léonide Massine's room. Between times, Picasso sketched portraits of his friends.

The war was still being fought at the time of the effervescence of this new spirit in which poetry, music, painting, and dance collaborated. What will be called *l'après-guerre*, the period after the war, made its start with *Parade*. Slowly, during the decade of the twenties, Cocteau's and Picasso's prestige grew and showered Paris with dazzling lights.

In 1917, *Parade* was a public scandal. Concerning that moment, Cocteau will say later: "From then on, I was to know only scandals, the notoriety of scandals, the luck and the bad luck of scandals." He often meditated on this aspect of his destiny. He returned to it and discussed it in his reception speech at the Académie Française.

Cocteau often referred to the two encounters at the beginning of his career which had a lasting influence on his life of an artist: the meetings with Igor Stravinsky and Pablo Picasso. *Le Sacre du printemps* affected him deeply. Stravinsky, first, taught him that unless art insults the habits of art, it remains a mere game. He quickly saw the many ways in which Picasso insulted the habits of art. The examples of Stravinsky and Picasso urged Cocteau to explain himself and to study the mechanics of his art.

Between Montmartre, where Max Jacob and Juan Gris lived, and Montparnasse with its café La Rotonde and Modigliani's studio, there was a constant traveling back and forth, supervised by Apollinaire, dominated by Picasso, and minutely observed by Jean Cocteau. This was the moment when stories about Cocteau, which quickly turned into legends, began to circulate. Most of them were absurd. Cocteau often said he was unable to recognize himself in the stories he heard. But even when the screen of legends is removed, a celebrated figure remains enigmatic. Cocteau often remarked that the artist is condemned to live as a phantom.

Picasso and Cocteau both preserved something from their childhood. And nothing is harder to preserve than one's childhood, its mystery and its wild cruelty. Almost all children, between the ages of five and ten, have talent for drawing. After that, in most cases, the talent is lost. In explaining this phenomenon, Cocteau used words that are almost untranslatable when he said: "What first carries children away ends by exiling them." (*Ce qui emportait les enfants les déporte.*) A child's genius is changed into a questionable talent, but the real painter rescues the chance granted to him as a child. Throughout his life, Cocteau did considerable drawing and painting, but for a long time he was afraid of painting. Picasso urged him to do this and made him feel ashamed of his fears. Many French poets have had a highly developed sense of graphic art and have left behind them drawings as additional works. Hugo, Baudelaire, Rimbaud, and Verlaine are examples of such poets. The three poets who were closest to Picasso: Apollinaire, Jacob, and Cocteau, were admirable graphic artists.

Painting by Cocteau, "The Slaying of Holofernes"

Cocteau's principal text on Picasso, published in the volume *Le Rappel à l'ordre*, counts today as one of the finest testimonials to the genius of the painter and as one of the most penetrating critical statements on the character of the creative genius in general. The essay is not easy to follow because Cocteau expresses himself as a poet. In it he speaks of the Muses as demanding ladies, accustomed to marked attentions. Often Cocteau observed Picasso trying to get beyond their domination, to move outside of their dance (*leur ronde*), as he says, but then Picasso would begin drawing like everyone else. So he returned quickly (so Cocteau reassures us) blindfolded and took up again his central position which is exactly within the dance of the Muses.

Cocteau looked upon Picasso as a Spaniard who had appropriated some of the oldest French recipes. These recipes are the works of Chardin, Poussin, and Corot. This Spaniard casts a spell over objects and faces that follow him wherever he wishes to go. First, Picasso tries out his spell on whatever is close at hand: a newspaper, a glass, a bottle, a pipe, a package of tobacco, a playing card, a guitar. In speaking of Picasso's art and Georges Braque's also, Cocteau claims that they debauch simple objects.

Picasso's earliest friends in Paris were Gertrude Stein, Guillaume Apollinaire, Max Jacob, André Salmon, and Maurice Raynal. Cocteau met Picasso a few years later and has written especially of the painter in his relationship with the theatre, as stage designer. The two men first knew one another during the rather austere period of cubism. Only the Spanish guitar and objects that are found on a table were permitted painters at that time, according to Cocteau. It was a crime to paint a stage set, especially one for the *Ballets Russes*. In accepting Cocteau's proposition for *Parade*, Picasso scandalized the café de la Rotonde. To put on *Parade*,

Cocteau and Picasso had to join Diaghileff in Rome, and the cubist code forbade any journey other than the Nord-Sud subway in Paris between la Place des Abbesses in Montmartre and le boulevard Raspail in Montparnasse.

Picasso appropriated the theatre as he had everything else. The night before the opening (la répétition générale) of Antigone, in December 1922, Cocteau and his actors were seated in the orchestra of Dullin's theatre, L'Atelier. On the stage there were openings on the left and right. There was an opening in the middle. Over this opening Cocteau had hung masks of women, boys, and old men. It was necessary to paint the surface of the panel. Picasso walked up and down looking at it. He began by rubbing a piece of red chalk over the panel which made it look like marble. Then he took a bottle of ink and traced a few elegant motifs. Suddenly he blackened a few spots and three columns appeared. The appearance of these columns was so abrupt, so unexpected, that Cocteau and his actors broke out with applause.

Later that evening when the two friends were walking in the street, Cocteau asked Picasso if he had planned on the emergence of the columns or if he himself had been surprised. Picasso replied that he had been surprised by them, but that one calculates often without realizing it, and that he had invented the column in the same way that the Greeks had discovered it.

When Jean Cocteau wrote for Paris-Midi his articles entitled Carte Blanche, he spoke of artists who were not known by the Paris public of that moment, 1920. The names which kept appearing in his chronicle were: Derain, Braque, Picasso, Apollinaire, Max Jacob, Erik Satie, and the group of composers called Les Six. These men usually refused publicly to take their art seriously, to speak seriously about their art.

They were especially distrustful of what might be called an explanation or an interpretation of their work. Their critical statements were almost always aphorisms, elliptical phrases, and condensations.

One day an American lady asked Cocteau to take her to Picasso's studio. She was the kind of woman who took delight in studying a variety of subjects: lessons in boxing, dance, gymnastics, singing, book-binding, history. She had once hired a teacher to help her read Mallarmé. Cocteau wondered if she had chosen him as teacher of cubism. Finally he refused to take her to Picasso, since he was well aware of how much the painter dreaded such encounters, and how useless he believed all explanations concerning art to be.

But one day the American lady told Cocteau, in a tone of triumph, that the painter Zuloaga had taken her to Picasso's studio. Cocteau asked her what had transpired. She explained that since Zuloaga was one of Picasso's oldest friends, the painter had made a clean confession. "Confession of what?" Cocteau asked. "That his cubism is a farce!"

For the publication of his play *Les Mariés de la Tour Eiffel*, in 1924, Cocteau wrote a preface which is really a manifesto, that today is still of great interest. It is an example of the critical texts about the new art in the century, those texts that are difficult to read, and that are rich in ideas and intuitions. According to this text, Cocteau's position did not conform with traditional disciplines, but it was in perfect conformity with Picasso's discipline. It was opposed to the esoteric and the mysterious, but was bent upon rehabilitating the commonplace. This work, both the preface and the text itself, was a new scandal, provoked by those who believed that the Eiffel Tower had been insulted. In *Le Coq et l'Arlequin*, Cocteau's aesthetics are still more apparent, as well as the significant affirmations concerning the morality of his poetics. In this essay is found the celebrated sentence on poets, in which Cocteau claims we shelter an angel whom we are constantly scandalizing. We should be the guardians of this angel. *(Nous abritons un ange que nous choquons sans cesse. Nous devons être les gardiens de cet ange.)* The artist is thus defined by Cocteau as being a man inhabited by another being.

Each element of the astonishingly varied work of Cocteau helps us to understand better the total work, and to understand better the period and the work of the artist friends such as Picasso. Cocteau as graphic artist has his place beside Cocteau the critic, the aesthetician, and the creator of new styles in the theatre and films. His book *Dessins* (1923) is dedicated to Picasso, and this dedication reveals an influence, although it is difficult to tell which was the stronger influence, the painter or the poet. It would seem that Picasso had contracted some kind of debt to Cocteau who, in 1917, traveled with him to Rome. Picasso's first "Greek" drawings and those in the style of Ingres possibly came after similar drawings of Cocteau. But such a question is vain and useless. It is more than evident, however, that Cocteau did not escape the marked influence of the Spaniard from Malaga whom he, as deliberately as Apollinaire did, placed in the foremost rank of contemporary artists.

In turning the pages of the album *Dessins*, crammed with surprises and variety, one is struck by the spirit, the tone of a period whose aspirations and whose taste are exemplified in *Les Ballets Russes, Le Sacre du printemps,* and Picasso's paintings. Somewhat later, in 1934, Cocteau published a series of illustrations for his novel: *Soixante dessins pour Les Enfants terribles.* These retell the novel graphically. In these drawings, Cocteau's art is closer to Christian Bérard's than to Picasso's. According to Cocteau, the book of pictures is intended to illuminate the literary text. Paradoxically, each is independent of the other, and each merges indistinguishably with the other.

It is difficult to separate Picasso from his poet friends, especially when one has in mind the extent of his influence on his century. Only today are we beginning to realize the incomparable richness of Picasso's Paris years. When Apollinaire died in the midst of the barbaric joy of the Armistice, the art world was severed in two. On one side, under the banner of Order: Claudel, Gide, and Valéry resumed and continued their work. On the other side was what seemed to be the Disorder of dadaism, futurism, and surrealism. Cocteau found his equilibrium mid-way between the order of Claudel and the disorder of Breton. But the lightness of his weight and his dexterity made those who watched, apprehensive. Would he fall?

Picasso and Cocteau, more than the other artists, retained through the years a youthfulness of spirit. Most poets and painters give the impression of pursuing the Muses, but, because of their determination, never quite catch them. But the Muses seemed to favor Cocteau and Picasso, and pursued *them*. Whenever one or the other was apprehended by the Muses, he would escape and this escape would be manifested in a new work or in a new painting.

To describe this type of artist, the image of a spring-finder (*sourcier*) has been used. And spring-finders are rare. They are men who, by means of a stick or a magic wand, discover fountains and springs. Cocteau's pen and Picasso's brush do bear resemblances to magic wands. Whenever they held them in their hands, refreshing water gushed forth in which objects were bathed. When the objects emerged from the bath, they appeared on the pages of the poet and on the canvasses of the painter.

Jean Cocteau and Pablo Picasso

They often chose simple objects of today, but they alone possessed the secret of endowing these contemporary objects with an ancient mythological character. Such power of renovation is a further sign of youthfulness. Cocteau and Picasso were involved with most of the vital artistic movements of the twentieth century, but they always remained independent of these schools. This will toward independence accounts for the unusual place they occupy in modern poetry and modern painting.

XI
EPILOGUE:
A MEETING
WITH COCTEAU

I T WAS in February 1960, a few days before I was to leave
Paris where I had been working for two months. During the
fifties, on two occasions, I had had reason to write to Jean
Cocteau, first, for permission to translate some of his poems
for an anthology, and secondly, for permission to undertake a
more ambitious project—the editing and translating of a
group of selected writings which I was to call *The Journals of
Jean Cocteau*. Patiently, and in the most friendly spirit, Cocteau guided me in his letters, counseled, and encouraged me.
The ease with which he welcomed me among his large number of correspondents, most of whom are concerned with the
study of some aspect of his work, delighted me, and I re-
sponded in a similar tone of friendliness tempered with the
strong admiration I have always felt for the man's accomplishments.

When I requested help in the choice of illustrations, Cocteau sent me folder after folder of drawings and photographs,

159

many of which I was able to use. He sent me three drawings as gifts: an early drawing based on *L'Après-midi d'un faune*, a drawing of himself at Oxford on the occasion of his receiving an honorary degree, and a drawing of two imaginary profiles, his and mine, separated by an ocean. Once in Paris, a mutual friend of ours brought me a very large drawing Cocteau had inscribed to me: a dog-unicorn with the face of Jean Marais, and a tent in the background and an heraldic inscription in the foreground.

These signs and these messages coming at intervals during three or four years, made it possible for me, in that February of 1960, when a New York publisher suggested I do further editing and translating of Cocteau, to write to him, with the hope that he might be in Paris at that time. I sent the letter to his Paris apartment, 36, rue de Montpensier. Three days later, early in the morning, a woman telephoned me *de la part de Jean Cocteau*. He was in Paris just for that day, and would I have lunch with him. I was to come to the apartment at one.

I was prompt in arriving. The door was opened by a smiling, elderly woman who greeted me with the words: "Vous êtes Wallace Fowlie. Je vous connais." I must have expressed surprise at her knowing me, and she continued with the cordiality of an old friend. "I was the one who mailed all the letters to you, and the photographs and the books. You see, I know you well, and M. Cocteau is delighted to see you today. He arrived last night from Saint-Jean-Cap-Ferrat, and this morning many many people have come by to see him. The last are with him now and you will have to wait a few minutes. I will put you in the small parlor." She had been guiding me during this speech of explanation toward *le petit salon*.

It was indeed small, a kind of secret alcove, whose walls were lined with dark red velvet. The window was concealed with the same velvet. Two photographs were on the wall: Rimbaud and Mallarmé. A small blackboard bore the familiar profile that Cocteau has drawn so many times. The room had a strange formal air, but the poets' photographs and the chalk profile (of Heurtebise?) put me at ease. Two or three times, during the next ten minutes, Madeleine (I learned later that was the housekeeper's name) opened the door to tell me it would be a few more minutes—and always added: *il y a eu un monde fou ce matin.* She was proud of this fact, proud that the man she served had attracted so many friends and visitors.

Then, at last, Cocteau opened the door and came in very quickly waving a paper in his hand. I had not realized the shortness of his stature and was unprepared for the visible signs of age on his face. Almost before greeting me, he explained the paper, a few lines he had just written which I was to use as a pass that afternoon to attend the first showing of his film *Le Testament d'Orphée.* Eighty-five friends had been invited for this private showing, and I would be the eighty-sixth! I accepted gratefully, but refrained from telling him I would be unable to go that afternoon. Then, with that first message dispatched, his face broke into a smile, and jovially he pressed my arms and shoulders: "Is it really you, in the flesh, after all that correspondence back and forth over the Atlantic?" It was a moment of youthful playfulness, a welcome which would have put anyone at ease.

"I am taking you to lunch," he said, "just around the corner at Le Véfour. . . ."

I had never heard of this restaurant, and therefore did not know it is one of the oldest and most celebrated in Paris.

Then Cocteau added, as a special inducement, "At my table, my name is on my chair, and Colette's place, similarly marked, is beside mine. We used to eat there together, two faithful inhabitants of the Palais-Royal."

As we left the apartment, I heard Cocteau say to Madeleine that he would be back by two-thirty for the next engagement, and Madeleine pointed to a black-board attached to the door, where evidently the day's schedule was written out, and said firmly, "Yes! no later than two-thirty!"

We walked then, at a fairly swift pace, to the restaurant in the Palais-Royal. Cocteau clung to my arm and talked all the way. Our entrance into the Véfour was impressive. Cocteau was surrounded and greeted warmly by the owner, the head waiter, the barman, two or three waiters, the lady cashier. It was a family welcoming him home. I stood aside, but with each new person he introduced me as *mon traducteur américain*. No one paid the slightest attention to that. He was the center and, as we slowly walked to the table, to his table, we were flanked by several attendants. He checked with the owner on whether he was planning to attend the showing that afternoon of *Le Testament d'Orphée*.

At the table, we stood for a moment, as Cocteau pointed out his name on the brass plaque on the back of his chair. And on the back of my chair, beside it, the name of Colette. "We ate here together on so many occasions," he said.

I knew of their long friendship, of the number of years when they were neighbors in the Palais-Royal section of Paris, and I remembered how Colette, stricken with bad arthritis during the last years of her life (she died in 1954), spent her days on a divan-bed, which she called her "raft" (*mon radeau*) and enjoyed the unannounced frequent visits Cocteau paid her. She used to say to him as he came in: "Assieds-toi sur mes pieds, Jean." As writers, they had almost nothing in common. Colette's clean prose was nourished on things, on their perfume and their form. Cocteau's poetry reflected myths and symbols. But in common they had many of the intangible values of life: an inexhaustible curiosity, a kindness of spirit, a profundity of sentiment. Their friendship was so well known it surprised no one when, at the death of Colette, Jean replaced her in the Belgian Academy.

When we were in our places, side by side, and as the maître d'hôtel handed us the large menus, Cocteau pointed out to me a center table and briefed me quickly: "You see, it's an old restaurant. Fragonard died at that table." And then, passing on to a practical problem, asked me if I would choose meat or fish for lunch. "Etes-vous homme à viande ou à poisson?" I chose a *sole* and he *rognons*. The wine waiter approached then, an elderly man who called Cocteau *maître* and whom Cocteau addressed by the familiar *tu*. I had noticed he used *tu* in speaking to everyone at the Véfour, from the proprietor to the bus-boy.

There was considerable discussion about the wine, because of my *sole* and Cocteau's *rognons*, but finally a half bottle of very light red wine was decided on, especially after I assured the two men I would drink very little wine. The elderly *sommelier* went off. Abruptly, Cocteau exclaimed that we could not begin with the main dish, and, calling back the maître d'hôtel, he ordered "six huîtres pour Jean Cocteau et six huîtres pour Wallace Fowlie." I had already noticed his tendency to speak of himself in the third person.

The two plates of oysters reached us almost immediately, and then the wine problem again became critical. I was aware that Cocteau rather enjoyed inflating the dilemma, and he was aware that I was aware. The wine steward was called back, and with the appropriate gesture and tone of voice, Cocteau explained that we could not drink red wine with oysters. I simply imagined that a half-bottle of white wine would eventually be ordered. But that was too predictable. Cocteau had been looking around at the other tables of which only three or four were occupied, at some distance from ours. "Don't you see," he said, "on those other tables large bottles of white wine that have been opened? Go over to one of them and ask for a small glass of white wine for Jean Cocteau and a small glass for his guest Wallace Fowlie."

The wine steward was as dumbfounded as I was. At the moment he could not assemble an answer, and Cocteau repeated his request and assured the old man that the guests would be happy to supply him with two glasses of their wine!

"Maître," began the wine waiter, "I know the state of your health, and I know it is unwise for you to have two kinds of wine at a meal. I have chosen for you a red wine so light that it can be drunk appropriately with oysters."

A tactful solution. Cocteau was visibly relieved, but the steward and myself were even more relieved.

"You are thinking I am poor," he said to me.

"That is impossible," I replied. "What about your book royalties and films and plays?"

"Yes, all of that is so carefully recorded that I have to pay taxes of sixty-three percent on my income. I am able to live thanks to the generosity of my good friend and benefactress, Mme Weisweiller. Most of the year I live in her villa in Saint-Jean-Cap-Ferrat, Santo-Sospir."

I had known of Cocteau's various addresses: the Paris apartment, the house at Milly-la-Forêt near Paris, and Mme Weisweiller's residence in the Alpes Maritimes. I asked him about the housekeeper I had just met. Madeleine had served him for several years. She was many things for Cocteau: housekeeper, secretary, guardian. She knew how to discourage the tiresome visitors and keep the schedule of important appointments when Cocteau was in Paris. This sturdy Burgundian was servant and friend at the same time, in her devotion and steadfastness. The Paris apartment was so small that she had to organize it carefully: Cocteau took his breakfast in the kitchen and it was there he visited with his friends, who had the habit of passing by in the morning. The tiny red parlor, where I had waited, was kept for more formal visitors. Madeleine used to call it *le salon des académiciens.* "But the next time," he said, "you will sit down in the kitchen." He had no way of knowing, and neither did I, that this was the only visit I would ever have with him.

"What are you working on now?" he asked me.

"I am translating two plays of Claudel."

"Don't bother with Claudel," was his swift answer. "Work on Jean Cocteau."

I smiled, but he did not, and finished his thought by saying: "Cocteau will last longer that Claudel."

I asked him what his relationship with Claudel had been.

"Very intermittent but always cordial. I called on him when I was making the rounds of the Académiciens, and I asked him if he would vote for me. He took my two hands in his, and said, 'Yes, Jean, with all my heart. But tell me one thing—why, in heaven's name, do you want to be a member of the Académie Française?' I tried to tell Claudel that such a move was so unexpected, that it was in keeping with my entire life."

Then I thanked Cocteau for the "pass" he had written out and given me to see the private first showing of *Le Testament d'Orphée.* I had read about the film. Already the literary weeklies were running articles and documentations on it. The topic was, of course, close to Cocteau's heart and he spoke of it at some length. He began by saying that I would see Mme Weisweiller in the film, in a scene shot in the garden of her villa at Saint-Jean-Cap-Ferrat. He had no subsidy for this film and had decided to use his friends for the various parts: actors, actresses, artists who gave him their time and talent. This meant he had to wait until something brought them to the south, to the region near Saint-Jean-Cap-Ferrat, and the two centers where most of the film was made: Les Baux-de-Provence and Villefranche. It was the culminating film of his career, the synthesis of his legends and themes.

Cocteau spoke, not rapidly, but steadily, and without transition from topic to topic. I no longer remember how he shifted from *Le Testament d'Orphée* to Mauriac. But Mauriac's name came up, and he spoke at some length of the man, and of his behavior at the première of *Bacchus*. I had seen a performance of *Bacchus* a few years previously, and I had collected all the articles and reviews of the Mauriac-Cocteau quarrel, the open letters and the discussions of the letters. The problems involved were not really on religion and morals. They represented a clash of temperaments. Cocteau felt this and I listened attentively to his analysis of Mauriac. In one of his typical, aphoristic flashes, which I don't believe he ever wrote down, he recapitulated the problem by saying quite simply: "You see, François Mauriac is the type of man who fundamentally does not like people. You and I do. . . ."

The dispute had been so public and so strenuous that Cocteau had believed a definitive break had been reached between him and Mauriac. Thus, at a subsequent large gathering, Cocteau was surprised when Mauriac sat down beside him and affably asked, "Alors, mon petit Jean, comment vas-tu?" "But I thought you had insulted me by your behavior at *Bacchus* and in print afterwards," was Cocteau's reply. "No, no, that was our literary side, the histrionics of the profession." "It was serious for me, however," said Cocteau, "and I had no intention of deceiving my public."

I was familiar with several of these stories that Cocteau related in the third person, but he often expressed a more personal attitude toward them than he had on the printed page. He spoke especially and fervently of Igor Stravinsky. In the middle part of their careers the two friends had been estranged, and their recent reconciliation had meant a great deal to Cocteau. He emphasized his conviction that Stravinsky is one of the very greatest artists of our day. Many years had gone by since Cocteau had written so movingly of *Le Sacre du printemps* and hailed it as a great turning point in contemporary music.

It was I who initiated the discussion about Jacques Maritain. Ever since the time of the two famous letters in 1926, letters that today have an important place in literary history, both Maritain and Cocteau remained faithful to their friendship. Cocteau's return to his faith in 1926, which he owed in part to Maritain, was expressed years later in the chapels he decorated. I had imagined, and I was right in this, that Cocteau's feelings for Maritain were as affectionate and loyal as ever. And so I told him of Maritain's fears that he might not be able to spend the last years of his life in France. I suggested that he take up this problem with André Malraux.

"Why just Malraux?" was his reaction. "I will telephone to De Gaulle, who admires Maritain and knows his work."

When I asked him if he knew De Gaulle personally, he replied in the affirmative, and said that only recently he had telephoned to him to say that De Gaulle was the first real anti-gaullist!

It was suddenly two-thirty, and I stood up as I reminded Cocteau that he had promised Madeleine to be back at the apartment at this time.

"But I want you to have another memory of Jean Cocteau in Paris. Tomorrow Mme Weisweiller and I go to Saint-Moritz. I have to go there periodically to build up my red corpuscles. For this trip I am having a woolen jacket made. Come with me to the store while I have a fitting. That will give us further time together."

Outside of the apartment, Mme Weisweiller's chauffeur

put us into the automobile and we soon drove up to Dior's. At the end of the store was a counter for men: ties, handkerchiefs, etc. And there we went. When Cocteau's name was announced, three tailors appeared from nowhere. The beige-colored jacket was tried on, and it seemed to me that in the space of a few moments, Cocteau indicated changes in almost every detail. As I watched him convince the tailors that he was right to ask for this and that change, I remembered his long career in the theatre where he was accustomed to assume responsibility for costumes as well as settings and mise-en-scène.

Satisfied at last that the instructions would be carried out, he turned to a salesgirl and said he wanted to pay her for a black tie he had purchased a month previously. She looked up the account. "Oui, en effet, M. Cocteau, vous me devez 5000 francs."

Cocteau opened his billfold, and, asking the young lady to extract from it the correct amount, explained in a good firm voice so that we all could easily hear: "I am confused over the new francs, and I don't want to give you too much or too little. The other day I was at Mougins at lunch with my great friend Picasso. His son came in and asked him for some money. When he took the bill his father gave him, he exclaimed, 'Mais papa, tu me donnes des millions.' "

As we walked back through the main part of the store, it was apparent that Cocteau's presence had been signaled to everyone. We walked through the gauntlet. Our farewell on the sidewalk was brief. He took out from his pocket a small gift which he gave to me and said that we would meet again at the end of the afternoon at Le Testament d'Orphée. "Orphée" was the last word I heard him say.

CHRONOLOGY

BIBLIOGRAPHY

INDEX

CHRONOLOGY

1889 Born July 5, at Maisons-Laffitte (Seine et Oise).

1899 After her husband's death, Mme Cocteau, with her three children, Jean, Paul, and Marthe, live in Paris, at 45, rue La Bruyère. Jean attends the lycée Condorcet.

1906 Edouard de Max reads Cocteau's poems at the Théâtre Fémina.

1912 Meets Serge de Diaghileff and Igor Stravinsky.

1913 Accompanies Stravinsky to Leysin, Switzerland.

1915 Friendship with the aviator Roland Garros. Meets Erik Satie and Paul Morand.

1916 Frequents Montparnasse, in company with Apollinaire, Jacob, Reverdy, Cendrars. Meets Picasso.

1917 Performance of *Parade*, at the Châtelet.

1918 Founds, with Cendrars, les Editions da la Sirène. Stravinsky quarrels with him because of *Le Coq et l'Arlequin*.

1919 Meets Raymond Radiguet.

1923 Death of Radiguet.

1925 Meets Jacques Maritain. Visits Villefranche. Meets Christian Bérard. Reconciliation with Stravinsky. Excommunicated by the surrealists.

1931 Illness at Toulon.

1936 Travels around the world.

1937 Helps the boxer Al Brown to recapture his title of champion.

1941 Moves to 36, rue de Montpensier in the Palais-Royal section of Paris.

1947 Occupies house at Milly-la-Forêt (Seine et Oise). Visits United States. Theatre tour in the Middle East.

1950 Decorates Villa Santo-Sospir, in Saint-Jean-Cap-Ferrat.

1955 Joins the Académie Royale de Belgique and the Académie Française.

1956 Honorary degree from Oxford. Paints frescoes of the Chapelle Saint-Pierre in Villefranche-sur-Mer.

1963 Dies October 11, at Milly-la-Foret.

SELECTED
BIBLIOGRAPHY

1. POETRY

Le Cap de bonne espérance. Ed. de la Sirène, 1919
Vocabulaire. Ed. de la Sirène, 1922
Plain-Chant. Stock, 1923
Poésie 1916-1923. Gallimard, 1924
L'Ange Heurtebise. Stock, 1925
Opéra. Stock, 1927
Léone. Gallimard, 1945
La Crucifixion. Morihien, 1946
Le Chiffre Sept. Seghers, 1952
Clair-obscur. Ed. du Rocher, Monaco, 1954
Paraprosodies. Ed. du Rocher, Monaco, 1958

2. NOVELS

Le Potomak. Société littéraire, 1919
Le Grand Ecart. Stock, 1923
Thomas l'imposteur. Gallimard, 1923
Le Livre blanc. Ed. des Quatre-chemins, 1928
Les Enfants terribles. Grasset, 1929
La Fin du Potomak. Gallimard, 1940

3. PLAYS

Parade. Rouart-Lerolle, 1919
Les Mariés de la Tour Eiffel. Gallimard, 1924
Orphée. Stock, 1927
Antigone. Gallimard, 1928
La Voix humaine. Stock, 1934
La Machine infernale. Grasset, 1934
Les Chevaliers de la table ronde. Gallimard, 1937
Les Parents terribles. Gallimard, 1938
Les Monstres sacrés. Gallimard, 1940
La Machine à écrire. Gallimard, 1941
Renaud et Armide. Gallimard, 1943
L'Aigle à deux têtes. Gallimard, 1946
Bacchus. Gallimard, 1952

4. CRITICAL WRITINGS

Le Coq et l'Arlequin. Ed. de la Sirène, 1918
Carte Blanche. Ed. de la Sirène, 1920
Le Secret professionnel. Stock, 1922
Le Rappel à l'ordre. Stock, 1926
Lettre à Jacques Maritain. Stock, 1926
Opium. Stock, 1930
Essai de critique indirecte. Grasset, 1932
Portraits-souvenir. Grasset, 1935
Mon premier voyage. Gallimard, 1937
La Belle et la bête (Journal d'un film). Janin, 1946
La Difficulté d'être. Morihien, 1947
Reines de France. Darantière, 1949
Lettre aux Américains. Grasset, 1949
Maalesh. Gallimard, 1949
Journal d'un inconnu. Grasset, 1952
Démarche d'un poète. Bruckmann, Munich, 1953
Poésie critique I. Gallimard, 1959
Poésie critique II. Gallimard, 1960

5. FILMS

Le Sang d'un poète (Music by Auric), 1932
Le Baron fantôme (Dialogue by Cocteau), 1943
L'Eternel retour (Music by Auric; scenario and dialogue by Cocteau), 1944
La Belle et la bête (Music by Auric), 1945
Les Parents terribles (Music by Auric), 1948
L'Aigle à deux têtes (Music by Auric), 1948
Orphée (Music by Auric), 1950
Les Enfants terribles (Scenario and dialogue by Cocteau), 1950
Le Testament d'Orphée, 1960

6. BOOKS ABOUT COCTEAU

Crosland, Margaret, *Jean Cocteau*. Peter Nevill, London, 1955
Dubourg, Pierre, *La Dramaturgie de Jean Cocteau*. Grasset 1954
Fowlie, Wallace, *The Journals of Jean Cocteau*. Midland Books, Indiana University Press, 1964
Jacob, Max, *Lettres à Jean Cocteau: 1919-1944*. Morihien, 1950
Lannes, Roger, *Jean Cocteau*. Seghers, 1947
Oxenhandler, Neal, *Scandal and Parade: the Theatre of Jean Cocteau*. Rutgers University Press, 1957

7. BOOKS CONTAINING CHAPTERS
    ABOUT COCTEAU

Bentley, Eric, *In Search of Theater*. Vintage Books, 1953
Fergusson, Francis, *The Idea of a Theater*. Princeton University Press, 1949
Fowlie, Wallace, *A Guide to Contemporary French Literature*. Meridian Books, 1957
Goffin, Robert, *Fil d'Ariane pour la poésie*. Nizet, 1964
Sachs, Maurice, *Le Sabbat*. Corrêa, 1946

INDEX

177